Believe Women

The Death of Due Process from Salome to #MeToo

Megan Fox

A Superversive Book

ISBN 9798606379491 (paperback)

Superversive Press

superversivepress.com

Published in the United States of America

CONTENTS

This book is dedicated to every man who has ever suffered because of the lies of a spiteful woman, and to every boy trying to grow up in a country whose women increasingly hate him for no other reason than his sex. It is unjust, it is corrupt, and it must not be allowed to go unchallenged. To every husband, father, and son, you deserve to have your innocence defended and due process honored.

FOREWORD

DEPLORA BOULE

Sometimes, it seems as though we're living through an unprece-dented moment in time, a scandalous page of history of which no one has ever seen the like. As we struggle in treacherous, uncharted waters, we are consumed with distrust, rage, and fear: distrust of everyone around us, rage against the unjustness of it all, and fear for the lives and wellbeing of ourselves and our loved ones. "Why me?" we rail in our minds. "Why must I be cursed to live through such uncivil times?" No ready answer comes, while all around us society roils and frays.

But sometimes, as we flail about on the storm-tossed sea, a ray of light breaks through the darkness, and a lifeline is tossed to us. We cling to it, test its veracity, cautiously trust its strength, then ravenously haul ourselves along its length until our feet rest once more on solid ground.

Today, the #MeToo movement is the devastating storm, and *Believe Evidence* is the lifeline.

#MeToo is the hashtag that launched a thousand mobs, the weaponized phrase of the internet age. It is the spark that lights the carefully-laid tinder of society's sleeper agents—ordinary people who have been mal-educated and indoctrinated to believe the greatest threat is people who don't think exactly the same way they do. These are the shock troops who wield social media, broadcast news, and baseball bats to destroy the target. They wreck people's lives without a glimmer of doubt that they are immaculately justified in their actions. They are The Mob.

I know what you're thinking; you're wondering what kind of people would name their child "Deplora Boule." The answer, of course, is no one; Deplora Boule is obviously a *nom de plume*, under which I write satire that mocks feminism and fake news. I don't use my real name, even though I already have a following from my previous works and would probably sell more books if I did. But I am afraid of The Mob.

There is a three-step process in place today by which the Left circumnavigates the legal standard of due process to dispatch its cultural and political rivals:

1. A member of a Victim Class invents a damning story about the target;

2. The establishment media runs with it and pounds the hate drum 24-7;

3. The Mob prosecutes justice. "Justice" in this case means neutralization of the target, whether it be through deplatforming and silencing, driving him/her out of a livelihood, or the sheer thuggery of intimidation, threats, and violence.

Everyone today is afraid of the mob. All one has to do is say the wrong thing, worship the wrong God, wear the wrong hat, or smile the wrong way to bring on the storm. The fear is as palpable as Salem circa 1692.

Fortunately, this is where Megan Fox throws us a lifeline. In *Believe Evidence*, Fox reminds us that there is nothing new under the sun. These times are in fact not only precedented many times over, they aren't even the worst iteration through which civilization has persevered.

In illustrative detail, backed by thorough research, Fox reminds us that there have been numerous instances of vindictive shrews throughout the ages. She cites Biblical-era "her-stories" like those of Jezebel and Salome, bloodthirsty battleaxes who thought nothing of wielding their female privilege to demand murder. We revisit Salem, circa 1692, where the hyperventilations of hysterical girls were enough to condemn innocents to excruciating deaths. We weep for the Scottsboro Boys in Depression-era Alabama, who lost the best years of their lives to the wicked, false manipulations of two strumpets. We relive the immoral outrage of race-baiting jailbait Tawana Brawley and her invented accusations against guiltless, uninvolved people. There are many additional examples, and in each case, we shudder with horror at the mob mentality that overtook otherwise sane societies.

Fox then neatly ties these infamous historical hoaxes to the contemporary moral panic of the #MeToo movement by pointing out copious parallels. She demonstrates that we're simply living through a case of history repeating itself, which is an oddly comforting fact. With the 20/20 vision of hindsight, we are reassured that things have been far worse before and that at some point this social upheaval, too, shall pass.

Finally, Fox goes one step further and issues sage advice for protecting children from the ravages of puritanical wrath. Her admonitions hail from the same era as the earliest cases presented in this book. The timeless rules for living a healthful, secure life that were first codified in Biblical times still hold the key to happiness today. Fox applies these practical techniques to modern childrearing, to help give our children (and our country) a future.

It is only through unawareness of the sordid past that history is able to inflict her most horrendous excesses upon mankind over and over again. With our schools now transformed into ignorance and rage factories, we are living in very dangerous times. Fascist mobs stifle liberty and dissent, socialism is yet again seriously considered, and misandry and bigotry openly shape public policy. As women claw their way to ever increasing power and fix men (especially young, white men) in their crosshairs, *Believe Evidence* becomes one of the most important books of our time. Indeed, the very title is an exhortation we all must heed if we wish to head off the catastrophic ends to which #MeToo madness is driving our society.

It's time to choose whether we will become yet another chapter in some future chronicle of murderous moral panics, or if we will once and for all learn the lesson that due process is a necessary component of any fair and civil society. I pray we choose the latter.

— Deplora Boule,
New York City,
February 2019

There is a troubling narrative that has taken over the national psyche summed up in one Twitter hashtag, #BelieveWomen. What began with the #MeToo movement, where women who had been sexually harassed in the entertainment field and subjected to the casting couch came forward, some with audio tapes, to expose criminal behavior by Harvey Weinstein, ended with wild, unfounded accusations hurled at perceived enemies to destroy them. The evidence presented against Weinstein met the legal standard to arrest and charge him with rape and put him on trial. Bill Cosby also was tried and convicted on the evidence brought forward by survivors of rape. It seemed that the #MeToo movement was a long awaited reckoning that would bring down the guilty.

The movement then morphed into the perverted idea that we must believe *all* women, who claim to have been sexually assaulted, even if they offer no evidence. It is enough, say #MeToo activists, that the women say they were assaulted and that they are telling "their truth." The idea that there is any other truth than the actual truth is terrifying in itself. We have proven ways of discovering truth in this country, and they don't include allowing each individual to have their own version of facts. #FactsMatter.

This seemingly new philosophy culminated into peak mass hysteria with the nomination process of Brett Kavanaugh to the Supreme Court, when Christine Blasey Ford came forward, at the last minute before the vote, to accuse him of sexually assaulting her over thirty years ago with no corroborating witnesses or evidence. While she succeeded in delaying the vote, when she finally testified (after lying about her fear of flying among other things), she didn't even claim to know when it happened, where she was, how she got home, or any other details that would help any investigator discover the truth. This lack of evidence didn't bother the Left in America at all. It was enough to whip up a mob of screeching harridans to destroy a man's entire life in the span of ten days. Anyone who dared to question Ford's account was labeled a misogynist. The senate confirmation process devolved into an inquisition into a 17-year-old's summer drinking habits, flatulence colloquialisms, and yearbook jokes. It was the lowest moment ever witnessed in American politics in my memory. Ann Coulter put it best when she said, "This is the closest thing we've ever had to Saddam's rape rooms. Bring a guy in and torture him in front of his wife, children & elderly parents. The left should be proud."[1]

I watched this spectacle with the mothers of America. We saw a good man, by all accounts and seven FBI background investigations, dragged through the mud, smeared, libeled, and defamed for political gain, and it terrified us. Without any evidence, and only the word of a woman whose own witnesses denied her account, Kavanaugh was fired from Harvard, denounced by Yale, and even faced uncertainty of whether he'd ever be able to coach his daughter's basketball team again. Expectedly, two other women came forward, one represented by the disgraceful Michael Avenatti (AKA Creepy Porn Lawyer who would later be arrested for domestic violence), to accuse Kavanaugh of even more ridiculous crimes, like gang rape and drugging women.

Even though those claims were dismissed as not credible by the FBI, and even NBC News, The Mob refused to acknowledge the obviously faked claims and continued to push them as credible. For the political gain of keeping a pro-life judge off the Supreme Court, there was no low to which the left would not go. This shameful smear job was perpetrated by sitting US Senators Feinstein, Booker, Harris, Schumer and others in a brazen, partisan hack-job. They predictably used their mob-for-hire of assorted freaks, like Antifa and the Women's March organizers, as the weaponized arm of the Democrat party to intimidate, harass, and scare Republican Senators. It was sickening. Ted Cruz and his wife were chased out of a restaurant, Lindsey Graham and Orrin Hatch were doxxed by a staffer in Sheila Jackson-Lee's office, which resulted in protesters banging on their doors all night long and threatening the safety of their families.

I looked at my son, who is only four, and began to wonder

how in the hell I could protect him from the screeching gorgon mobs who might come for him one day, if he rose too high on the wrong side. I wasn't the only one. Mothers across America reached out to me, terrified, sad, and bewildered. Sarah Hoyt, author and fellow writer at PJ Media, wrote of her son's experience with lying, malicious girls at school who accused him falsely of sexual harassment. [2]

> The background was this: 18 girls, most of them children of the staff, had decided my son was – and I'll use their term – "retarded" and therefore"dangerous" And they'd decided to make us remove him from the school/get the school to expel him by accusing him of "harassing them." [They said he] FOLLOWED THEM HOME, throwing rocks and threatening them, on a day I'd picked him up in the car. (In fact, I started making a practice of this. Which is why one day, parked under a tree, I watched my son leave the school pursued by one of these delicate flowers who was throwing rocks at him and calling him filthy names.)

The entire piece is a must read to understand the depths of damnable deception to which women and girls can sink in order to get their way.

Nowhere in the press could anyone find tales of despicable women, hell-bent on destroying men for a grudge or personal gain. All we were treated to was the constant drumbeat that women are honest and credible, and we should blindly believe all of them. *Puhlease.* This book had to be written to combat the outright lies about the nature of women and of what great evil they are capable. Throughout history and literature, there is no shortage of true, and fictional, tales of duplicitous and downright evil women, who intentionally destroyed the men in their lives for selfish reasons. I aim to knock down the claim that women today are somehow changed or elevated beyond the usual human frailties and are, in fact, subject to the exact same skepticism with which we should view all accusers. The burden of proof is always on the accuser to prove her case. The very foundation of our nation depends on looking at each claim in a rational and orderly way, on demanding evidence of criminal behavior, and on the presumption of innocence, and due process. Without it, this great nation will dissolve into anarchy, and your sons, husbands, and fathers will pay a steep price.

"The liar is no whit better than the thief, and if his mendacity takes the form of slander he may be worse than most thieves. It puts a premium upon knavery untruthfully to attack an honest man, or even with hysterical exaggeration to assail a bad man with untruth."

— THEODORE ROOSEVELT

PART I

HYSTERICAL
HARPIES
THROUGHOUT
LITERATURE
AND
HISTORY

EVE

No account of the duplicitous nature of women would be complete without mentioning Eve of the Bible. My mother used to read me great Bible stories at bedtime and so my knowledge of biblical examples of female treachery is vast. For those readers who are of the atheist or agnostic persuasion, the allegories presented from the Bible are still extremely relevant to discussions of human behavior. At the very least, these books are historical records kept by the Jews and early Christians and accepted as a timeline of these two peoples. What we can learn from them is every bit as relevant as Shakespeare, Homer, or other great books. The account of Adam and Eve, whether you view it as fictional or historical is still relevant to the subject.

At the beginning of the story, Adam and Eve are careless and content. Eve was the culmination of Adam's existence. His problem of loneliness was solved forever with God's gift of this perfect woman, his crowning achievement of creation. At the moment he sees her, Adam becomes a poet.

"And the rib that the Lord God had taken from the man he made into a woman and brought her to the man. Then the man said, 'This at last is bone of my bones and flesh of my flesh; this one shall be called Woman, for out of Man this one was taken.'"[1] There is no doubt this woman was greatly esteemed by Adam. One can almost feel his awe of her. She is his reason for living from that moment on, but then things go terribly wrong.

The serpent, Satan, gets the woman alone. Why did he go to the woman instead of attempting to corrupt Adam? This may be the most important question for our purposes of discovering what is the true nature of woman. Is it possible that the serpent knew he would get nowhere with the man unless he used the woman? The serpent knew that Eve could make Adam heel. Eve was the weapon of mass destruction that was used against man. This powerful position is the natural state of women. Men don't like to hear it, but it's true. If a woman wants something from a man, she's going to get it. This is not always done through evil or manipulative ways but women know how to use their natural gifts of feminine persuasion to attain their goals. We are born with it. You know it, I know it, and if you're a man, you surely have experienced it (for good or bad). My daughters can get their father to do things for them I would never do. Their wiles don't work on me, but they work on their father like a drug. And this is natural and good most of the time. The relationship between men and women is a mysterious and beautiful thing. When each is acting within moral boundaries, there is no end to the joy that comes from male and female love, familial or romantic. Girls learn about this power within them early! Watching a two year old girl bat her lashes at her Daddy for an extra treat is fascinating to witness. They hone these skills on their fathers before they take them into the world and use them on potential mates.

The serpent recognized Eve's power over Adam and knew he had to harness it to turn it against him. It was brilliant. Going to Adam would have been boring. It may have worked, but it wouldn't have had the same deep betrayal or drama, or created the rift between man and woman that his scheme accomplished. After the deed is done, God turns to Eve and declares that she will now suffer pain of childbirth, but that's not the worst of it. Worse, He says, "your desire shall be for your husband and he shall rule over you," and it is still so.

Some have called it the Battle of the Sexes, but it began with the fall of man that started with Eve. We are now destined to continue that struggle against one another until the end of time. No matter how many advancements women make in a world of men, he shall always rule over us because it was so ordered by God (or if you prefer, nature). It is the rage-filled rebellious spirit of woman screaming at God for this punishment that we heard on the Supreme Court steps during the Kavanaugh confirmation process. Women who have accepted this fact of life and human sin live much more peacefully with men than those who don't. Radical feminists appear to want to place men underfoot and squash their natural authority in all things. This will never come to pass because it is not the natural state of mankind. They can cry and scream and rage and protest but it will not change basic human nature. And it was a woman who brought it to pass through allowing herself to be used by evil to destroy man. Throughout the human story, this scenario repeats over and over again, confirming woman's deep resentment of her master and the lengths to which she will go to destroy him.

ATHALIA

*Now when Athaliah, Ahaziah's mother, saw that her son was
dead, she set about to destroy all the royal family. But
Jehosheba, King Joram's daughter, Ahaziah's sister, took
Joash son of Ahaziah, and stole him away from among the
king's children who were about to be killed; she put him and
his nurse in a bedroom. Thus she hid him from Athaliah, so
that he was not killed; he remained with her six years, hidden
in the house of the Lord, while Athaliah reigned over the
land.*[1]

Imagine the evil in the heart of a grandmother who
could order the deaths of all her grandchildren in
order to retain the power of the throne. This evil act of sacrificing
children for a woman's advancement and power cannot be better
illustrated in the modern times that what's happening behind

Planned Parenthood's doors. The descriptions of the abhorrent practices of the pagans is laid out in plain terms in many places in the Old Testament. Child sacrifice is a well-documented practice of ancient peoples.

> The Lord spoke to Moses, saying: Say further to the people of Israel: Any of the people of Israel, or of the aliens who reside in Israel, who give any of their offspring to Molech shall be put to death; the people of the land shall stone them to death. I myself will set my face against them, and will cut them off from the people, because they have given of their offspring to Molech, defiling my sanctuary and profaning my holy name. And if the people of the land should ever close their eyes to them, when they give of their offspring to Molech, and do not put them to death, I myself will set my face against them and against their family, and will cut them off from among their people, them and all who follow them in prostituting themselves to Molech.[2]

The ancient Canaanites and other nations who practiced child sacrifice believed they could not be blessed by their gods without it. Killing infants wasn't their only vice, only one of many that included complete sexual "liberation" including bestiality, incest, pedophilia and any other sexual deviancy imaginable. None of these things are new but always embraced by people who reject God's laws as written by Moses. These days, you don't have to look far to find similar women killing their own children for their own selfish gain or sexual freedom. A vast majority of abortions are done for convenience of the woman. The Guttmacher Institute conducted a study in 2004 that found "among the structured survey respondents, the two most common reasons were 'having a baby would dramatically change my life' and 'I can't afford a baby now' (cited by 74% and 73%, respectively—)."[3] Modern child sacrificers believe it's justified to kill a child for the advancement of the woman, in other words, if it keeps her from ruling over her kingdom then send in the butchers. And so, like the ancient pagans, today's feminists cry out in a loud voice "kill them!" even up to the moment of birth. In the state of NY, full term abortions are now legal and in Virginia a similar bill was narrowly defeated after its proponents were unwisely honest about it in front of cameras.

The reason that Judge Kavanaugh has been slandered and defamed by hysterical women is because they fear one thing; losing their ability to kill their children. Abortion is a sacrament to the left as religious in meaning as the eucharist is to Christians. Abortion is the act through which radical feminists retain their power and avoid sacrificing themselves for someone else. Instead, they put on the altar their own children so they can have momentary relief from inconvenience and trouble. It is also a political weapon with which they wield over women as a threat, promising poverty and death if their blood god is not appeased. They keep women in a state of false fear of "back alley abortions" (that never happened in great numbers as claimed) and financial ruin. Contrary to the claims that women were dying en masse to the tune of 1000 to 5000 a year from illegal abortion, the CDC reported that in 1973, the same year Roe v. Wade was decided, only 39 women died from illegal abortion. Perhaps not surprisingly an almost equal number also died from legal abortion the next year. [4] But lying has never been an obstacle for the radical feminists. Alternatives to abortion, like adoption, are not even considered in the minds of the "choice" movement. Abortion is a major means of controlling a voting block through fear and deceit. Lie about what it is (blob of cells) and when it is viable (20 weeks) and what the complications can be (death, depression), then threaten freedom itself while petting women's natural vanity and selfish human nature, and you have a recipe for a hot button issue with which to control masses of women. (It is important to note that abortion is still extremely unpopular among a majority of Americans who favor more restrictions, but the hysterical harpies make all the waves.[5]) They will never give up abortion without a major fight, as we have seen. Their power is too important to them and, like the ancient pagans, they believe they won't receive the blessings they are owed in life if they have to put their desires second to the desires of another.

Is it any wonder the pro-abortion left will rally behind any woman who fights against their major foe, a pro-life Supreme Court Justice, using whatever means necessary including lies? Do not be fooled that any "Women's March" is anything but a giant pro-abortion march. Masquerading as a parade of strong women protesting the president's supposed treatment of women, the march is full of hypocrites. Supposedly, based on locker room comments, said in jest to Billy Bush about how some women throw themselves at wealthy famous men and *let* them grab them by the nether regions, the Women's March claims to be outraged at the mere mention of a man admitting to being very sexually active with willing women (while pretending he was talking about sexual assault). From that silly off-handed (and true) comment about gold-digging women, the rabid left put together national marches aimed at embarassing the president for his remarks in an unguarded moment. The irony here is, of course, that the same women who pretend to be affronted by the word "pussy," run around with depictions of vulvas on their heads, holding signs that say "Grab this pussy!"

The feminists have, for years, encouraged everyone to get rid of old sexual morals and chase the "big O" at all costs! No marriage was sacred enough to save, no institution grand enough to withstand the sexual Pandora's Box the feminists unleashed on us like a wrecking ball. Pretending now, after instituting sex-ed that would make a hooker blush in kindergartens across America, that they are offended by a sexually active man using the word "pussy," is just bonkers. These are the same people who dress up in giant vagina costumes and go out in public, like they're perfectly normal. They host "Sex Week" on college campuses and hire porn stars to teach your freshmen student how to use sex toys attached to power tools. No one is buying that the sex-crazed feminist left got the vapors over hearing a guy talk about his sexual conquests. This is pure political posturing. Proving my point, these nasty women immediately took to the streets, wearing hoohas on their heads, to protest the use of the word "pussy."

Female genitalia, coincidentally, is heavily symbolic in pagan fertility worship. The parallels between the ancient child-sacrificers and the modern ones just keep appearing! There are hundreds, if not thousands, of ancient pagan fertility goddesses depicted with over- exaggerated vulvas and breasts like Inanna, a Sumerian goddess and Lajja Gauri, a Hindu goddess. The women's marchers are just an extension of the ancient fertility cults who partook in horrific acts for personal gain. If women are willing to kill their own children is there any depravity too distasteful in which they won't participate?

JEZEBEL

Has there ever been a more wicked woman than Jezebel? She whose name lingers, used by feminists unironically on their ranting blogs, is known even to the irreligious. They have taken her name without realizing what they have done. For surely, in all the Bible, there is not a more infamous name than Jezebel. Murderer and blasphemer, idolatress and prophet killer, she was so feared that the mighty Elijah himself, who could command bears to devour his enemies, ran and hid rather than stick around waiting for the hell she promised to unleash on him.

Jezebel was married to a weak king of Israel, Ahab. Ahab was a man who knew God but followed his she-devil wife into worship of Baal. He allowed two of his sons to be sacrificed at her demand. Jezebel made it her business to kill the prophets of God who would dare tell her she was doing wrong and leading Israel into sin. Elijah hid one hundred prophets from her in the desert and spent much of his time avoiding her wrath. What led to Jezebel's rage was a hilarious incident between her prophets and Elijah. Elijah once mocked Jezebel's prophets of Baal in a ceremony where they put their gods to the test. While the pagans were wailing and cutting themselves and crying out to their deaf, dumb, and blind god to send fire to their altar, Elijah stood there and yelled insults at them, asking them if Baal was possibly on the toilet having a moment, or perhaps on vacation. After an exhausting effort, the pagans gave up. With one command, Elijah brought down the fire of heaven which consumed even the water soaking the altar. Completely humiliated, the pagan prophets returned to Jezebel and whined about what Elijah did to them.

The worst thing anyone can do to a pagan is laugh at them. They hate it so much they want you dead. So began Jezebel's killing spree against the prophets of God who had owned her pagan priests on top of that mountain. If that spectacle had been broadcast today, it would be on the Comedy Network as a roast special.

I often reference this story when Christian people chastise me for using ridicule against the pagan Left. It is not true that God's people must always be quiet as church mice and accept the cultural rot we find ourselves stewing in. We are supposed to point out the absurdities of sin and death culture. And if we can do it with humor, so much the better! Jesus did it all the time. He had some of the sharpest comebacks ever.

Why do you see the speck that is in your brother's eye, but do not notice the log that is in your own eye? Or how can you say to your brother, "Let me take the speck out of your eye," when there is the log in your own eye? You hypocrite, first take the log out of your own eye, and then you will see clearly to take the speck out of your brother's eye. [1]

That's funny and effective stuff. Ridicule works. The best weapon we have against the humorless left is to laugh at them. They hate it so!

After Jezebel's prophets were mercilessly ridiculed by Elijah, she had ordered her soldiers to hunt down and kill him and the prophets of God. Meanwhile, King Ahab was worrying about gardening. He decided he wanted a vineyard next to his palace owned by a man named Naboth. Naboth refused to sell it to him because it was his family inheritance. The sullen king made a fine display of his unhappiness about the matter at home, sulking and pouting until Jezebel, exasperated, demanded to know what was wrong with him. Upon learning that his tantrums stemmed from this run in with Naboth, Jezebel berated her husband for his stupidity and weakness. She challenged his manhood and his status as a king. Ahab was clearly a Gamma male who had long before turned over his natural authority to his shrew wife. Jezebel insulted him for a while (as harpies do) and then told him to buck up and be happy because she was going to solve this problem for him, *as usual.* What she did next is breathtaking in its wickedness.

So she wrote letters in Ahab's name and sealed them with his seal; she sent the letters to the elders and the nobles who lived with Naboth in his city. She wrote in the letters, "Proclaim a fast, and seat Naboth at the head of the assembly; seat two scoundrels opposite him, and have them bring a charge against him, saying, 'You have cursed God and the king.' Then take him out, and stone him to death." The men of his city, the elders and the nobles who lived in his city, did as Jezebel had sent word to them. Just as it was written in the letters that she had sent to them, they proclaimed a fast and seated Naboth at the head of the assembly. The two scoundrels came in and sat opposite him; and the scoundrels brought a charge against Naboth, in the presence of the people, saying, "Naboth cursed God and the king." So they took him outside the city, and stoned him to death. Then they sent to Jezebel, saying, "Naboth has been stoned; he is dead."[2]

This murderous siren actually fabricated evidence in order to have a man killed! And just like all mob justice, there was no one to stand up and speak for him, to deny that what the accusers said! Instead, they took him out and killed him with nothing but public accusation. Shortly thereafter, Ahab took possession of the vineyard of the man his evil wife had set up for destruction. These two did not get away with their crimes. Ahab died in battle, and, as prophesied by Elijah, and dogs lapped up his blood. Jezebel's death is probably the most satisfying death of a devilish harpy ever written.

When Jehu came to Jezreel, Jezebel heard of it; she painted her eyes, and adorned her head, and looked out of the window. As Jehu entered the gate, she said, "Is it peace, Zimri, murderer of your master'" He looked up to the window and said, "Who is on my side? Who?" Two or three eunuchs looked out at him. He said, "Throw her down." So they threw her down; some of her blood spattered on the wall and on the horses, which trampled on her. Then he went in and ate and drank; he said, "See to that cursed woman and bury her; for she is a king's daughter." But when they went to bury her, they found no more of her than the skull and the feet and the palms of her hands.[3]

Good riddance! The dogs devoured Jezebel before the men could bury her. It's just so fitting an end to a treacherous woman with no regard for life or honor. It feels like justice, something we lack in modern society. Under our current system it appears that women who come forward and accuse a man with false information and kill his reputation, walk away unscathed and even more prosperous with book deals and GoFundMe accounts. I rather like the "eaten by dogs" ending myself, but maybe that's just me.

Julie Swetnik, the lying harpy who accused Brett Kavanaugh of facilitating "gang rapes" by putting drugs in drinks, should at the very least be put in prison (if we can't find dogs to eat her). Her story is so fake, not even the major news media that traffics in fake news could make it sound reasonable. In her first interview, she contradicted her written statement and had to admit that she didn't know if Kavanaugh was drugging anyone or standing in line to rape anyone, but he was handing out Solo cups, (and that's basically the same thing).

"During the years of 1981-82, I became aware of efforts by Mark Judge, Brett Kavanaugh, and others to 'spike' the 'punch' at house parties I attended with drugs and/or grain alcohol so as to cause girls to lose their inhibitions and their ability to say 'No,'" she wrote in her legal statement under penalty of perjury. Shortly into her interview with NBC, Swetnick changed this story to saying she had witnessed Kavanaugh handing out cups to girls. "Did you see Brett Kavanaugh spiking the punch?" asked the NBC interviewer. "I saw him giving red Solo cups to quite a few girls during that time frame, and there was green punch at those parties, and I would not take one of those glasses from Bart Kavanaugh, I mean, Brett Kavanaugh, excuse me!" replied the lying liar. "I saw him around the punch...containers. I don't know what he did," Swetnick continued, licking her lips nervously with a forked tongue.

NBC opened the interview stating, "There are things [Swetnick] told us on camera that differ from her written statement last week. We have been trying independently to reach out to anyone who remembers attending parties with Julie Swetnick and Brett Kavanaugh...so far we've not found anyone who remembers that." Irresponsible reporter Kate Snow continued, "She's also unclear about when she first decided to come forward."[4] Considering all these things, any worthwhile investigative journalist would never have gone ahead with this stupid interview the minute they discovered that her on-camera story contradicted her written statement. The only right thing to do with it at that point was turn it over to the FBI and police for investigation into false allegations. NBC didn't do that.

What have we come to when we allow contemptible liars to walk away scot free after smearing an innocent man simply because the accuser has a sweet smile and XX chromosomes? Our ancestors did not have this problem. *Instead they threw the lying wretch out of a window, trampled her with horses, and then ate a hearty meal celebrating her demise!* That's justice.

POTIPHAR'S WIFE

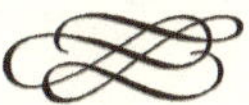

Poor Joseph. This guy could not get a break. He went from being a favorite son with an awesome coat to a victim of human trafficking. Worse, his brothers sold him into slavery and told his father he got eaten by animals. (*And you thought you had a dysfunctional family?*) While in slavery in Egypt, Joseph got an important assignment working for a wealthy and connected man named Potiphar. Potiphar was so impressed by Joseph that he gave him full reign over his house and all his affairs. But there was one problem. Potiphar's wife was a harpy whore from Hell.

In the book of Genesis, we learn that this dame-in-heat tormented Joseph daily, begging him to have sex with her while her husband was away. Joseph put the Mike Pence rules into action way before Pence thought of them. He flat out refused her advances and then decided to never be alone with her until one fateful day he had business in the house and didn't know she was waiting for him, like a poisonous spider.

Now Joseph was handsome and good-looking. And after a time his master's wife cast her eyes on Joseph and said, "Lie with me." But he refused and said to his master's wife, "Look, with me here, my master has no concern about anything in the house, and he has put everything that he has in my hand. He is not greater in this house than I am, nor has he kept back anything from me except yourself, because you are his wife. How then could I do this great wickedness, and sin against God?" And although she spoke to Joseph day after day, he would not consent to lie beside her or to be with her. One day, however, when he went into the house to do his work, and while no one else was in the house, she caught hold of his garment, saying, "Lie with me!" But he left his garment in her hand, and fled and ran outside. When she saw that he had left his garment in her hand and had fled outside, she called out to the members of her household and said to them, "See, my husband has brought among us a Hebrew to insult us! He came in to me to lie with me, and I cried out with a loud voice; and when he heard me raise my voice and cry out, he left his garment beside me, and fled outside." Then she kept his garment by her until his master came home, and she told him the same story, saying, "The Hebrew servant, whom you have brought among us, came in to me to insult me; but as soon as I raised my voice and cried out, he left his garment beside me, and fled outside."

One wonders if she used her scared little girl voice like Dr. Ford did when relaying her tall tale. Potiphar believed his floozy wife over Joseph and threw him into prison for attempted rape where he stayed for years. This story resonates for several reasons. English playwright and poet William Congreve famously wrote, "Heav'n has no rage, like love to hatred turn'd, Nor hell a fury, like a woman scorned." Throughout all of time, man has known (or learned very quickly) that rejecting a woman is a very dangerous endeavor. We will never know what conspired between Dr. Ford and Judge Kavanaugh, if anything. Upon listening to her testimony, it seems clear she knew who he was and was, at least peripherally, around him at times. What seems most likely is that Kavanaugh, popular football player, never noticed her despite her best efforts and that may have been his only crime. In the eyes of a sullen teenaged girl, this rejection could have morphed into a toxic stew of hatred and desire for revenge. If she saw him as responsible for making her feel rejected, unwanted, or uncool by his inattention, a mentally unstable person could turn that into assault. By her own testimony, she admitted to being in therapy for several years. We did not learn about what mental conditions she's been diagnosed with or what medications, if any, she has been prescribed. For all we know, she could be a bonafide psychopath!

Dr. Ford's version of events, that she was assaulted at a party by Brett Kavanaugh, was uncorroborated by her own witnesses including her best friend who had no recollection of being at any such party with Kavanaugh or Judge. My best friend and I met in high school, too. The two of us could corroborate our whereabouts at every memorable party that we attended. One doesn't just forget about parties where your best friend was assaulted. It's far more likely that the party never happened.

The problem with women who feel wronged to the extent that Potiphar's wife and Dr. Ford did, is that they will say anything and do anything to get back at the "cause" of their distress. Dr. Ford's testimony read like the diary of a teenage stalker. At one point, she talked about seeing Kavanaugh's friend Mark Judge at a local Safeway and that he was "extremely uncomfortable" at seeing her. If that did happen, is it possible Judge was uncomfortable around her because she was a socially awkward girl who kept trying to hang out with him and his friends? The answer is yes! It's completely possible that Dr. Ford made up a scenario in her mind that never happened because the truth is too embarrassing. But we can't know because we have no time machine, and the press is doing their best to keep Ford's life a total mystery. We know everything there is to know about Brett Kavanaugh including what was on his 9th grade calendar, what his inside jokes with his friends were, his friends' nicknames and fart jokes, but we know nothing about what kind of girl Dr. Ford was.

Unlike Potiphar's wife, who was smart enough to grab some evidence that made her story at least plausible, Ford had nothing, not even the testimony of her best friend who she claimed was there. Note to future bearers of false witness: Make sure you get at least one piece of worthwhile evidence in your quest to destroy a good man because without it, there's little hope of getting away with it.

Potiphar's wife succeeded in ruining Joseph for a while, but she did not stop him from rising to one of the highest positions in Egypt eventually.

Pharaoh said to his servants, 'Can we find anyone else like this—one in whom is the spirit of God?' So Pharaoh said to Joseph, "Since God has shown you all this, there is no one so discerning and wise as you. You shall be over my house, and all my people shall order themselves as you command; only with regard to the throne will I be greater than you." And Pharaoh said to Joseph, "See, I have set you over all the land of Egypt." Removing his signet ring from his hand, Pharaoh put it on Joseph's hand; he arrayed him in garments of fine linen, and put a gold chain around his neck. He had him ride in the chariot of his second-in-command; and they cried out in front of him, "Bow the knee!" Thus he set him over all the land of Egypt. Moreover Pharaoh said to Joseph, "I am Pharaoh, and without your consent no one shall lift up hand or foot in all the land of Egypt." Pharaoh gave Joseph the name Zaphenath-paneah; and he gave him Asenath daughter of Potiphera, priest of On, as his wife. Thus Joseph gained authority over the land of Egypt.[1]

It's fitting that Brett Kavanaugh has also been elevated to one of the most powerful positions in our land after suffering the false accusations of a vengeful woman. (I refuse to call uncorroborated allegations "credible" like some kind of GOP weak-spined talking head suffering from Tourette Syndrome. It was preposterous how fast even the conservative press raced forward to declare Ford "credible." The word "credible" was so overused it became comical. Uncorroborated allegations are, by definition, not credible in the least and should be considered untrue until proven otherwise by solid evidence.)

SALOME

Though not much is said about Salome in the Bible, her actions had dire consequences for John the Baptist. John the Baptist was the forerunner to Christ, Jesus's blood cousin, son of Elizabeth who was a relation of the blessed Mother, Mary. He was considered the greatest prophet to have ever lived. He was described as a wild man who lived in the desert, subsisting on insects. Like all good prophets, he spent most of his time speaking truth to power and confronting those living in sin with their crimes against God and imploring them to repent.

John's final act was to tell Herod Antipas to stop having sex with his brother's wife, Herodias. It's interesting that the great prophets were often concerned with publicly denouncing those who were committing sexual sin. A tell-tale sign of paganism was the extreme sexual disorder that accompanied it, including incest, fertility rituals, bestiality, and homosexuality. All of these things were specifically outlawed by God who spoke to Moses in the desert and carved his law into stone.

If you were ever curious about the Christian reasons for the limits imposed on sexuality, the example of Herodias couldn't be more instructive. Christians believe that natural laws exists for our own good and health. We know now that incest breeds birth deformities and illness, bestiality is simply cruel, and the secret no one in the LGBTQWTF community want you to know is that the act of anal sex is extremely damaging to the health of the colon and surrounding tissue. It is a scientific fact that those who practice anal sex are at greater risk of HIV, anal prolapse, fissures, bowel infections that can lead to painful death, and high rates of HPV that causes anal cancer.

The *LA Times* called anal cancer the "next gay epidemic." "The American Cancer Society estimates there will be 8,200 new anal cancer cases in 2017. In the absence of national screening recommendations, more than fifty percent of these individuals will be diagnosed at stage III or IV, when five-year survival is less than forty percent. This creates a major public health concern," they reported.[1]

Within the article was a link to another story about a study that was done showing that women who engage in anal sex also have a higher risk of anal cancer.[2] This led to the obvious conclusion that anyone, male or female, engaging in anal sex is participating in high risk behavior that is dangerous to their health. Shortly after I reported the findings on *PJ Media* with what they left out (that anal sex increases risks of HPV), the *LA Times* threw that article down the memory hole. The link is now dead. Luckily, my report can still be read.[3]

There is a concerted effort by media, for ideological purposes, to hide the truth of the dangers of anal sex from the public in order to make the gay community seem attractive, which only endangers lives. Meanwhile, we are expected to accept rosy how-to guides initiating teen girls into the "pleasures" of anal sex as taught to them by Planned Parenthood sex "educators" at public schools we are forced to fund through property taxes (taxation is theft!).

When Christians say that God's way is life, it's because we know that living contrary to the laws of nature will always lead to physical pain and spiritual death. If you know that certain behaviors will harm people, and you are a man of God like John the Baptist, you have an obligation to tell them. That's exactly what the prophets of the Bible did. They risked death by telling the uncomfortable truth. We are living in an age where men of the cloth are risking leading their flocks to Hell to avoid being socially beheaded for proclaiming natural law.

Father James Martin comes to mind. He is a man who could not be more opposite of John the Baptist. Well-groomed and soft spoken with smooth hands and squishy demeanor, he travels around the country proclaiming that the Church's teaching on homosexuality isn't authoritative because it hasn't been accepted by the gay community. He calls everyone to love their gay neighbors without trying to help them to live according to God's law. While he's 100 percent correct that we should love all our neighbors and not chastise or correct them, a minister of the Church cannot possibly take that route without serious consequence. Isn't the entire job of a shepherd to herd the flock? I fully expect that if I am openly engaging in mortal sin that my priest, like John the Baptist before him, is going to pull me aside and tell me to stop. As a Christian, I would need to accept pastoral correction and repent. His job is not to cheerlead me through sin, but to help me out of it. Sometimes that takes direct confrontation, which should only be done by a pastor. The rest of us need concentrate on our own stuff. And this point needs underlining because of the delicate nature of the topic and the unfair label Christian people get of being "hateful" or "homophobic." Christian people don't hate gays. They love them and want the best for them. They want them to be happy and healthy and whole.

Milo Yiannopoulos was interviewed by the Jesuit *American Magazine* edited by Fr. Martin, and they refused to print it so he released the interview on is own. It's not surprising that Fr. Martin did not want to publish Milo's strong defense of traditionalism as Martin spends his life trying to change the fundamental teaching of the Catholic faith on sexuality. "You don't see me disputing the Church's teachings on homosexuality," wrote Yiannopoulos. "There's no intellectual tension, because I wouldn't dream of demanding that the Church throw away her hard truths just to lie to me in hopes I'll feel better about myself. I love the truth, not lies, and I know no one's feelings are the basis of truth. That's why I don't understand those Catholics — such as, if you'll forgive my horrid impertinence, this magazine's editor at large, Fr. Martin — who imply that if people don't like what the Church says, maybe the Church is wrong or should apologize. The Church was founded on a rock and a cross, not on a hug."[4]

The Catholic Church has always taught that only homosexual acts are sinful, but the attraction is not. These days, though, even priests are muddying the issue. When the man of God refuses to step up to the plate and correct his flock, what is the point of even having him? John the Baptist had no such squeamishness and he paid for it with his life. Perhaps that's why many fail to speak out —simply repeating magisterial teaching that has remained the same for 2000 years is social suicide.

At that time Herod the tetrarch heard about the fame of Jesus, and he said to his servants, "This is John the Baptist. He has been raised from the dead; that is why these miraculous powers are at work in him." For Herod had seized John and bound him and put him in prison for the sake of Herodias, his brother Philip's wife, because John had been saying to him, "It is not lawful for you to have her." And though he wanted to put him to death, he feared the people, because they held him to be a prophet. But when Herod's birthday came, the daughter of Herodias danced before the company and pleased Herod, so that he promised with an oath to give her whatever she might ask. Prompted by her mother, she said, "Give me the head of John the Baptist here on a platter." And the king was sorry, but because of his oaths and his guests he commanded it to be given. He sent and had John beheaded in the prison, and his head was brought on a platter and given to the girl, and she brought it to her mother. And his disciples came and took the body and buried it, and they went and told Jesus.[5]

What's absolutely evident here is that confronting people about sexual sin is one of the most dangerous tasks there is. Sexuality has become an identity so that when sexual behavior is discussed, a person who identifies as his sexuality becomes unwilling to hear any criticism of it because it's an attack on "who he is." But this identity is false! We are not our sexuality. If you are a Christian your only identity should be "Christian." All other things are secondary. This is very similar to people who insist on hyphenating their nationality like "Italian-American" or "African-American" when the reality is we are just Americans and in union with one another because of that shared heritage. Dividing into identity groups separates people.

One of the main disciplines in the church is the call to chastity, to which all are called, even married people. If you're ever interested in more on that subject, look it up sometime because there are reams written on the call to chastity and what it means for everyone. Gay Christians are called to exactly the same chastity expectations as straight Christians. One of the best sources for more on the subject is the catechism of the Catholic Church.

All the baptized are called to chastity according to their state in life. Those who profess virginity or consecrated celibacy must give themselves to God with an undivided heart. Others (single or married) live chastity by their state. Married people practice conjugal chastity. Single people must practice continence. "There are three forms of chastity - that of the spouses, of the widows, and of the virgins. We do not praise one to the exclusion of the others," (St. Ambrose)."[6] Remaining faithful and resisting temptations require adopting the needed means: self-knowledge, self-discipline, obedience to God's commands, moral virtues, and prayer. "By chastity, we are led back to the unity from which we were fragmented into multiplicity" (St. Augustine). Chastity allows reason to permeate the passions and sensual appetites.[7]

This mastery over passions is imperative in all aspects of the Christian life! How else do we avoid gluttony, wrath, envy, sloth, lust, or any other forbidden thing? It's daily hard work. When we don't master our passions, it leads to horrific things like murder, as evidenced by Herodias's and Herod's illicit relationship that they refused to control. Herodias was a woman living in a disordered, incestuous relationship with her husband's brother. In fact, Herod had divorced his wife in order to have Herodias. These two were committing open, incestuous adultery. Perhaps not surprisingly, Salome ended up marrying her uncle. These people were in slavery to their sexuality. So when they were confronted by the evil of what they were doing, instead of repenting, they plotted to murder the messenger.

Salome was clearly put up to the murder by her scheming mother who was tired of hearing John chastise her for who she loved. Instead of considering whether what she had done had hurt her former husband and daughter, she sent Salome out to dance for Herod on his birthday. This is yet another strange example of the incestuous nature of pagan life. What kind of mother would have her young daughter dance for her step-father? Herodias was one *creepy crone*. Some say the dance wasn't sexual, but there's no way to know. Considering the machinations these people went through to continue living in adultery it seems highly likely that it was provocative. And the reward for this strange dance was to have a man's head lopped off and brought, bloody and dripping, to Salome on a platter. I suspect she delivered the gruesome gift straight to her mother for her approval. Women who are enslaved to their passions will do horrendous evil to continue serving their insatiable master.

LADY MACBETH

William Shakespeare could write a terrible shrew. Such was Lady Macbeth, murderess and instigator, teetering on the edge of insanity. Early in the play we see that Lady Macbeth is a contemptuous woman who is bent on achieving power through murder which she laments she cannot do herself, needing her husband to step up and berating him until he does.

> *What beast was't, then,*
> *That made you break this enterprise to me?*
> *When you durst do it, then you were a man;*
> *And, to be more than what you were, you would*
> *Be so much more the man. Nor time nor place*
> *Did then adhere, and yet you would make both:*

They have made themselves, and that their
  fitness now
Does unmake you. I have given suck, and know
How tender 'tis to love the babe that milks me:
I would, while it was smiling in my face,
Have pluck'd my nipple from his boneless gums,
And dash'd the brains out, had I so sworn as you
Have done to this.

This woman is terrifying. The image of her crushing the skull of her suckling babe should have been enough to tell Macbeth he should have her locked in the dungeon immediately. But instead, he allows her to upend his opinion of himself as a man and agrees to murder the king and pin it on innocent men to prove himself to her. Be on guard, gentlemen. Women can and have manipulated men into countless horrific acts of murder.

All one must do to verify that fact is watch any episode of *Snapped*, a true crime show, of which I am a great fan, that highlights female killers. Anyone who watches even one episode should forever banish the misconception that women can do no evil. Sharee Miller is a Lady Macbeth of the modern age. Miller recently sent a letter from prison, where she sits for arranging the murder of her husband, admitting to the crime of destroying two men. "I knew [the murder] was going to happen and I allowed it. I allowed a man to kill another man based on my lies and manipulation," she wrote.[1] Miller manipulated her ex-lover, a former police officer, into murdering her husband. The lover eventually shot himself and left a confession which put her in prison for life.

This lethal woman killed two men without getting a drop of blood on her. Beware the manipulation skills of women. They are a potent drug to the male constitution.

The very first question that should be asked of women, wagging their tongues with sinister plotting is "How now, you secret, black and midnight hags? What is't you do?" Rest assured, many women that men meet with regularly are hunched around a cauldron cooking up a poisonous stew with which to kill, maim, and destroy. Be not fooled by duplicitous witches. This side of women should not surprise anyone. We shrink from Lady Macbeth's description of dashing her new babe into a bloody mess but sigh helplessly while hordes of women get their babies chopped up and sucked out of the womb totaling over 200,000 a year[2], chalking it up to their "choice" and ignoring the bloody baby parts in red hazmat bags behind the clinics.

Abortion is a horror instigated by women and forced on men through manipulation. Most men accepted it readily, escaping responsibility, while others feel the deep sting of the child they wanted but could not save. The women responsible for this took away father's rights with a scribble of nine judges' pens. Fathers are fathers no more without the consent of mothers. It is a tyranny of the matriarchy yet unmatched in history in its cruelty. Nothing matters more than the will of the woman, regardless of whether she destroys a man and a child in the process. It is horrific. She forces her mate to partake in the bloodletting, covering both of them in the blood of the innocent. "What hands are here! Ha, they pluck out mine eyes. Will all great Neptune's ocean wash this blood clean from my hand? No, this my hand will rather the multitudinous seas incarnadine, making the green one red," laments Macbeth, upon returning from the sick stabbing of the king. And even crying out to her in pain, Macbeth can get no sympathy from his savage wife. "My hands are of your color, but I shame to wear a heart so white," she mocks, calling the man who just committed murder for her a coward. And it's true that any man who would allow a woman to manipulate him to such an evil act has forfeited his birthright of dominance and opted for cowardice and subservience instead. A strong, morally upright man would have turned her into authorities from the first confession of her hideous plan. But men can be weak where women are concerned, choosing their affection for them over common sense, and it could be argued that women such as these choose the weaker men as their targets. This gives moral women more urgent responsibility to diligently raise sons with stout hearts, able to stand for right and good and against the wiles of corrupt women. It's up to us to warn them what beastly plots lie in wait for an unsuspecting and vulnerable man.

"Fair is foul and foul is fair," the cry of Macbeth's witches, is a battlecry of our current times. All one has to do is look around at our rotting culture to see it in play. For Macbeth, what was supposed to be fair that turned out to be foul was his treacherous wife. Today, nearly everything that was once deemed good we are told we should believe it to be bad. There was a time when sex and children didn't go together in America, but now you're a homophobic bigot if you don't want some creep in your kindergarten class telling your kid what anal sex is. Men in the ladies' room or locker rooms was always seen as a reason to call 911, but not anymore! We've evolved so far that any 8-year-old who complains about seeing a penis in the girls' room is a bigot, but if an 19-year-old sees a penis at a college party, that's grounds for a senate investigation that could ruin a man's life! A man retaining his innocence until proven guilty used to be the very height of justice until the screeching hags of feminism decided that accusers should not be forced to bear the burden of proof anymore because, *feelings*. Up is down, black is white, fair is foul and all of us suffer it. "Ah, you who call evil good and good evil, who put darkness for light and light for darkness, who put bitter for sweet and sweet for bitter! Ah, you who are wise in your own eyes, and shrewd in your own sight!"[3]

Macbeth and his psychotic queen finally meet a tragic end. Lady Macbeth is tortured by a mental break that leaves her unable to sleep, walking the hallways in the middle of the night trying to scrub blood off her hands until she "by self and violent hands, took off her life." Macbeth is so focused on his quest to become king he barely notices her violent end before he is killed in a fight. It is likely that all affection for her died the night she drove him to murder an innocent man, aborting the innocence within him. Women who play these games with their power, using it in fiendish ways to attain superiority over men deserve the natural consequences that come, be it jail or death. Lady Macbeth was tortured by the knowledge of her treachery. One can only hope those women who "get away" with murder are either repentant and changed or haunted by their corruption night after night, tossing in agonizing sleeplessness, unable to scrub the guilty stain of death from their souls.

ABIGAIL WILLIAMS

No book about malicious women who harmed men would be complete without the story of John Proctor. Proctor was executed in Salem, Massachusetts in 1692 with fourteen women, four men and two dogs for the crime of witchcraft. For our purposes here, we will look at Arthur Miller's play, *The Crucible*, for the telling of his story, details of which have been changed somewhat to fit Miller's vision. But Proctor was a real man who suffered the torture of his son, and was executed for a crime which he did not commit all on the word of a malicious liar, Abigail Williams. Miller once wrote,

"People were being torn apart, their loyalty to one another crushed and…common human decency was going down the drain. It's indescribable, really, because you'd get the feeling that nothing was going to be sacred anymore."[1] While Miller was referring to the McCarthy senate hearings that searched for Communist spies within the arts community, the feeling he described is indistin-guishable from the current state of our country after the Kavanaugh senate circus. (The one major difference, of course, is that McCarthy really did find commie spies which KGB records confirmed years later. In Kavanaugh's case, no such records or evidence was found.)

Instead of hunting commies, Democrat senators scoured in vain for a drunken, 17-year-old rapist. In a way, the Brett Kavanaugh they were trying to question didn't exist at all. How does a man, removed some 35 years from his former child-self, answer questions directed to the child? The whole thing was absurd. It felt like watching what a senate hearing might be like if you had dropped a hit of acid before-hand. It had all the same features of a disorienting hallucination, screeching women (some of them bleeding on themselves), fainting protesters, trapped people in elevators, senators being chased down hallways, the distant sounds of chanting, and people on the news claiming you didn't see what you just saw with your own eyes in the form of an extremely implausible witness everyone called "credible" a million times before lunch. Senator John Kennedy, a Republican, called it an "intergalactic freak show," which was right on the money. I never thought I'd live to watch a future Supreme Court justice have to testify under oath, "I liked beer. *I STILL LIKE BEER*," as if beer were meth and everyone on the senate committee were teetotalers who never partied with Ted Kennedy.

Christopher Bigsby, who wrote an introduction to *The Crucible* in 1995, must have had some kind of time machine to see into our future where a senate confirmation hearing was turned into a modern day Salem witch trial.

> In our own time we are not so remote from this phenomenon as to render it wholly strange. Men and women with no previous memory of assaults, which were apparently barbaric and even demonic, suddenly recall such abuse, more especially when assisted to do so by therapists, social workers, or religionists who offer themselves as experts in the spectral world of suppressed memories. Such abuse, recalled in later life, is impossible to verify, but the accusations alone have sufficed to destroy entire families. To deny reality to such abuse is itself seen as a dangerous perversion, just as to deny witchcraft was seen as diabolic in Puritan New England.

Dr. Ford's supporters act the part of the outraged Puritans demanding that we believe the accuser's every word or we are complicit in crimes. We are the damned. Yet, they offer no evidence, and rational people everywhere must demand evidence before lynching a man. Otherwise, the only thing left to us is a swinging gallows heavy with innocent bodies. Lindsey Graham so hilariously and rightly pointed out the futility in continuing to try to prove the impossible, "Let's dunk him in the water and see if he floats," he quipped to nearby shrieking women in the Senate building hallways. What else could we do if we throw out evidentiary procedure? Cast runes? Play tarot cards? What modern feminists are asking reasonable people to do is become completely unreasonable, irrational feel-monkeys with no regard for civility or law. We've seen how this worked out in Salem, and none of us want to go back there. It's not an exaggeration to say that the Salem witch trials were one of America's most shameful examples of a total collapse of justice. We need to revisit what happened there to make sure it is never repeated. It's terrifying how close we came during Kavanaugh's confirmation process. Bigsby concludes his introduction writing, "However, not only do accused witches still die…but groundless accusations are still granted credence, hysteria still claims its victims, persecution still masquerades as virtue and prejudice as piety."

I never saw a more pious crew than the senate Democrats lined up one by one to interrogate a man about youthful drinking and yearbook jokes as if they were uncovering Al Capone's secret vault. And much like that unfruitful endeavor, they came up empty. After dragging a man's name through the mud for a solid two weeks without giving him a chance to speak up for himself, they all sat in wide-eyed horror as Judge Kavanaugh unleashed righteous anger on them in his opening statement. The drumbeat went out from that moment to then accuse him, not of rape, but of a poor judicial temperament! It would be funny if it wasn't so evil.

John Proctor had a similar outburst when the town lackey came to take his wife who was being accused of witchcraft by the wicked liar Abigail Williams. "If she is innocent! Why do you never wonder if Parris be innocent, or Abigail? Is the accuser always holy now? Were they born this morning as clean as God's fingers?" Does this not describe how the press treated Dr. Ford? None of them tried to find out what was on her social media, that was mysteriously scrubbed, or in *her* yearbook. Not one major media outlet tried to discredit her or poke holes in her story. Any journalist with a grain of integrity would have at least tried to find out if she was lying. Instead, we were treated to breathless reporting on St. Christine the Brave, the doctor without sin, who is now a role model for women everywhere and who, at the time of this writing, is being given an honorary degree from her alma mater. Feminists everywhere have constructed altars in her likeness in front of which they cast their spells to bind Judge Kavanaugh's loins. (This is not a joke. They're doing this.)[2]

"I'll tell you what's walking Salem," says Proctor. "Vengeance is walking Salem. We are what we always were in Salem, but now the little crazy children are jangling the keys of the kingdom, and common vengeance writes the law! This warrant's vengeance! I'll not give my wife to vengeance!"

Little crazy children indeed. Is that not what we all witnessed taking over the streets of Washington D.C.? Crazed women behaving like children demanded vengeance against Kavanaugh for the crime of who knows what (was it tugging on a bathing suit?) and drinking beer. And each day it continued as more insane women came forward to accuse him with more otherworldly accounts each nuttier than the next. "He drugged girls!," "Rape trains!" "Solo cups!" "Flasher!" and so on ad nauseum. Where was the law in all of this? Where was probable cause? Where were responsible journalists who would not print unsubstantiated garbage? They were all too busy fainting over specters and spirits they insisted were floating around on the ceiling that the rest of us couldn't see.

After Dr. Ford's interminably long testimony, where she was petted and assuaged at every turn and never questioned on anything seriously (like why she claimed she feared flying in the press but had absolutely no problem traveling to exotic locations all over the world for vacations), it finally came time for Judge Kavanaugh to speak. As he walked down the hallway gripping his wife's hand, I saw thunder in his face and utter despair on hers. The two of them looked as if they had been through Hell, and surely they had. I can't imagine having to tell your ten-year-old daughter not only what "gang rape" is but that her father had been accused of it on television.

Proctor's response to the court officers who dragged his wife away in the middle of the night struck me as especially pertinent in relation to Judge Kavanaugh's performance at his hearing. "I will fall like an ocean on that court. Fear nothing, Elizabeth," cried Proctor as they were dragging his wife away in chains.

The ocean did fall in a spectacular way on the senate kangaroo court. Senator Feinstein and her array of flying monkeys weren't prepared for the category five hurricane that Kavanaugh was about to set loose onto the despicable rats sitting opposite him.

Eleven days ago, Dr. Ford publicly accused me of committing a serious wrong more than thirty-six years ago when we were both in high school. I denied the allegation immediately, unequivocally, and categorically. The next day, I told this Committee that I wanted to testify as soon as possible, under oath, to clear my name. Over the past few days, other false and uncorroborated accusations have been aired. There has been a frenzy to come up with something—anything, no matter how far-fetched or odious—that will block a vote on my nomination. These are last-minute smears, pure and simple. They debase our public discourse. And the consequences extend beyond any one nomination. Such grotesque and obvious character assassination—if allowed to succeed—will dissuade competent and good people of all political persuasions from serving our country.[3]

Not only did Kavanaugh passionately defend himself from false allegations but he put forward a solid defense of the law itself. If we dispense with due process, the whole system we have built will collapse on itself. Neighbor against neighbor, husband against wife, mother against child, the chaos and horror is too terrible to contemplate. And yet, we've seen this before. We all were assigned *The Crucible* in grade school, were we not? It is a work so important that up until recently, when English teachers threw it out in favor of gay love stories and transgender coming out tales, it was required reading for all American school children. It's a cautionary tale, not an instruction manual, and yet it reads like a play by play of the Kavanaugh hearing. Like John Proctor, Kavanaugh also had a letter signed by 200 people he knew claiming that he was a person of good moral character and had never treated any women they knew with anything but respect. Proctor also showed a similar letter to the court showing ninety-one character witnesses for his wife. Instead of believing all women, both courts decided that only the women telling fantastical fabrications were worthy of their belief.

Even the questioning by the morally-retarded Democrats[4] mirrors the questioning in Proctor's hearing.

Senator Sheldon Whitehouse: Let's look at "Beach Week Ralph Club biggest contributor." What does Ralph mean?

Brett Kavanaugh: That probably refers to throwing up, I'm known to have a weak stomach.

Senator Sheldon Whitehouse: The next one is uh, Judge have you, I don't know if it's 'buffed' or 'boofed,' how do you pronounce that?"

Brett Kavanaugh: That refers to flatulence. We were 16... If you want to talk about flatulence at age 16 on a yearbook page I'm game.

Sen. Whitehouse: Devil's Triangle?

Brett Kavanaugh: Drinking game.

Sen. Whitehouse: How's it played

Brett Kavanaugh: Three glasses in a triangle. Ever played quarters?

Sen. Whitehouse: No.

Cheever: When I spoke with Goody Proctor in that house, she said she never kept no poppets. But she said she did keep poppets when she were a girl.

Proctor: She has not been a girl these fifteen years, Your Honor.

Hathorne: But a poppet will keep fifteen years, will it not?

Proctor: It will keep if it is kept, but Mary Warren

swears she never saw no poppets in my house, nor
anyone else.
Parris: Why could there not have been poppets hid
where no one ever saw them?
Proctor, *furious*: There might also be a dragon with
five legs in my house, but no one has ever seen it[5]

It's almost uncanny how well these two transcripts just flow together isn't it? I can't be the only one who sees the detestable Abigail Williams in Dr. Ford. How tiring it is to hear of her goodness everywhere you turn! John Proctor surely sickened every time that stupid judge would stop the proceedings to question Williams lovingly about whatever apparition she was claiming to see at the moment. Proctor knew her to be a conniving whore who was out to murder his wife and yet, even with evidence no one would listen to him.

I felt much the same way watching Dr. Ford give her sly testimony, dripping with irritating vocal fry and valley girl up notes at the end of every sentence. If you closed your eyes, it sounded as if you were listening to an 18-year-old sorority girl being interviewed on the street about topics she'd never heard of, not a 60-year-old doctor of psychology. What kind of person with a doctorate doesn't know the meaning of the word "exculpatory?" It never rang true to me. She sniffed a lot and broke her voice at times but never did an actual tear fall. Never did her skin become blotchy with emotion nor did she choke back sobs. In fact, it was bizarrely unemotional peppered with strange laughing and smiling as everyone in the room treated her like a mentally handicapped pet, giving her breaks every 7 minutes or so. Senator Booker even raced to her side to bring her coffee himself, not even allowing a staffer to do it! Such theatrics! They fawned over her like beaus at a picnic with Scarlett O'Hara. And the end result of her testimony was that she couldn't say when the party was, where it was, who was there, or how she got there or home. Her best friend denied her account, claiming she wasn't there and has never met Brett Kavanaugh. There was zero evidence to support Ford's claims, and yet, half of the country worships it as gospel.

There is, however, plenty of evidence that a man's name has been destroyed because of Dr. Ford's claims. Kavanaugh's emotional statement about his reputation and the burden to his family brought tears to many eyes. "As predicted, my family and my name have been totally and permanently destroyed by vicious and false additional accusations," he said, choking on actual sobs.

At the end of *The Crucible*, Danforth is pressuring Proctor to sign a confession which he refuses to do. When asked why, Proctor explodes at him, "Because it is my name! Because I cannot have another in my life!...I have given you my soul; leave me my name!" A man has very little in life but his reputation. If that is destroyed, no fruit of his life's work means anything.

The Democrats' smear job was so complete that the only thing Brett Kavanaugh was left fit to do was sit on the Supreme Court! Had he been denied that seat he would have been returning to a life of total expulsion! During the proceedings, he was fired from his teaching job at Harvard because the screeching womyn's studies majors cried that they felt "unsafe" with him on campus. A particularly horrible piece of reporting in *USA Today* said "The

U.S. Senate may yet confirm Kavanaugh to the Supreme Court, but he should stay off basketball courts for now when kids are around,"[6] not so subtly suggesting that Kavanaugh is a child molester! This man wasn't even going to be allowed to coach high school basketball after the Democrat smear machine was through with him.

The only comfort in the story of the Salem witch trials is that the experience was so horrible, so unjust that the power of the theocratic courts were broken forever, and the government stepped in to shut it down. The victims families were paid restitution, but it did little to right the damage done to the innocent people who lost their lives. We can only hope that the spectacle of ruining the Kavanaugh name was so unjust, that it will break the #MeToo overreach and cause the general public to demand evidence from any future accusers before allowing the hysterical crazy feminists destroy another person. It does seem to have lit a fire in the previously jelly-spined GOP to stand up to these disgusting tactics and fight against the tyranny of the mob and stand up for the rule of law.

MAYELLA VIOLET EWELL

The left has always loved *To Kill a Mockingbird*. Who doesn't? But the left just adores Atticus Finch. They seem to think loving this book says something about how *not* racist they are or something. The truth is, it's a wonderful book and a scathing rebuke of everything Democrats have become. Atticus Finch is what "liberals" used to be. I refuse to call anyone on the Left a "liberal" because they are so severely illiberal about absolutely everything. They have become statists with totalitarian tendencies who chase people out of restaurants and bars because they disagree politically crying "fascist" and "punch a Nazi!" wherever they go. It's embarrassing, and it isn't "liberal" behavior at all.

Atticus Finch is the type of person they see themselves to be, but in fact are the glaring opposite. Finch, the brilliant small town lawyer, defends Tom Robinson, a black man accused of raping a white girl, Mayella Ewell, in 1934. This was no easy thing. He suffered death threats, stood up to lynchers, public attacks, and persevered through it all because he was on the right side of the law and morality.

His closing arguments to the jury could have been read in front of the senate confirmation hearings for Brett Kavanaugh![1]

> To begin with, this case should never have come to trial. This case is as simple as black and white. The state has not produced one iota of medical evidence to the effect that the crime Tom Robinson is charged with ever took place. It has relied instead upon the testimony of two witnesses whose evidence has not only been called into serious question on cross-examination, but has been flatly contradicted by the defendant. The defendant is not guilty, but somebody in this courtroom is. I have nothing but pity in my heart for the chief witness for the state, but my pity does not extend so far as to her putting a man's life at stake, which she has done in an effort to get rid of her own guilt.

Mayella was a sad and pitiable character. Abused by her drunken father and left to fend for herself with seven children and no help, she was doing what she had to do to survive. She had to tell her father that Tom attacked her. If he knew the truth, that she tried to come onto a black man, he probably would have killed her. Even so, Mayella's situation does not warrant more sympathy than Tom's. He is the wronged party by a mile. There are few who don't feel some pity for Dr. Ford. She doesn't seem like the brightest bulb in the pack, and Diane Feinstein has unclean hands in the release of her initial letter that said Ford did not want the information in it to become public. Someone in Feinstein's office leaked it to the press against the wishes of Ford. But like Finch so wisely put it, I don't feel sorry enough for her to put a man's life in the toilet simply on her word alone. No. We need evidence, please.

There is another part of the closing argument that I would like to replace the word "negro" with "man" and "white" with "woman" to illustrate how accurately this narrative tells our modern happenings. For what was the prejudice against black people in our country has been replaced with deep misandry and bigoted attitudes against men.

> And so a quiet, respectable, humble **man** who had the unmitigated temerity to 'feel sorry' for a **woman** has had to put his word against two **women**. I need not remind you of their appearance and conduct on the stand--you saw it for yourselves...in the cynical confidence that their testimony would not be doubted, confident that you gentlemen would go along with them on the assumption--the evil assumption--that all **men** lie, that all **men** are basically immoral beings, that all **men** are not to be trusted around our women, an assumption one associates with minds of their caliber.

It's uncanny. The man-hatred (and especially white male hatred) that has taken over the Left is so great that the same women who were trying to knock down the doors of the

Supreme Court with their bare hands went home and started taking out their rage at losing the smear war on their own husbands and lovers who voted for Obama! Two articles popped up in the aftermath with truly unbelievable tales. Amy Butcher at *Literary Hub* penned an essay titled *MIA: The Liberal Men We Love.*[2] What was in it had me laughing so hard I saved it on a PDF so I can refer back to it whenever I need a pick-me-up.

> To a certain extent, we expected it from the men who wear lobster-printed pants, the men from Connecticut, the Young Republicans of America with their gelled and parted hair, their summers in Nantucket, their LL Bean slippers worn on the porches of fraternities, 2pm on a Monday. But when my friend pulls me aside in a hotel bar and tells me it's happening to her husband—a man who donates annually to NPR and voted twice for Barack Obama, who has a degree in Art History and works for a non-profit—neither one of us knows what to say.
>
> We speak of it like an infection: has it spread to your household yet?...Everywhere across America, liberal unions once so strong in love—relationships founded on mutual respect and trust and commitment and loyalty—have found themselves upended, or at the very least foundationally rocked, by the political escalation as it relates, perhaps most specifically, to womanhood and gender. Twenties or thirties or forties, children or no children, married or engaged or committed via long-term relationships: I have met more women than I can count in these past three weeks alone who have confided, in low voices—or once shouting, disbelieving, desperate, we have

three children, one woman cried to me—of the disruption in their own home.

It only gets better from there. She continues,

My husband worries about our daughter, she told me recently. That I'm only teaching her she's a victim. One day, while she was picking their children up from daycare, he burned a handful of her possessions: her Nasty Women shirt, her Hillary Clinton pins. My husband filed for divorce, another confided a few days later. He said he loved me and shared in some of my frustrations, but "could no longer tolerate," he said, the level at which I felt them. Hours later, another wrote to tell me of a save-the-date no longer in need of saving. My fiancé called off the engagement, she wrote. He loves me—he's sure, and I believe him—but he's "overwhelmed" with everything and "doesn't know how to comfort me" and "doesn't love who I've become..." He's from a very liberal family, the former fiancée said to me, baffled. And he is very liberal himself, which is why this is so alienating. I'm noticing, admits another, that a lot of liberal men especially are finding it difficult to deal with the current feminist movements. I'm frustrated and embarrassed, my boyfriend of three years said to me, with how worked up you are. He didn't find palatable my rage, the anger I felt for Trump, for the men and women who voted for him, was in fact embarrassed that I led 90 students from my small Ohio university through the streets of Washington with half a million Americans...and when I returned, delirious for sleep but feeling righted, in some small way satiated, he stood there in the hall and told me he was overwhelmed. All of you women with your labia hats, he said. All of you with your clitoris signs. The March, it seemed to him, was half a million people coming together in a collaborative act of inefficiency. Our anger was unpalatable—more than that, it was a waste. He shared in our frustration, agreed Trump was an embarrassment, a terrible man, but found himself exhausted by the outrage and activism borne of contemporary feminism.

It appears to have never occurred to these women that men don't find screeching, angry females fun to live with. *Shocking.* Then there was this article in the Washington Post by Victoria Bissell Brown called, "*Thanks For Not Raping Us All You 'Good Men' But it's Not Enough*" that ran in the *Washington Post.*[3] This woman reaches levels of moonbattery that should be recorded for posterity and used to teach the young women what not to do to your husband.

I yelled at my husband last night. Not pick-up-your-socks yell. Not how-could-you-ignore-that-red-light yell. This was real yelling. This was 30 minutes of from-the-gut yelling. Triggered by a small, thoughtless, dismissive, annoyed, patronizing comment. Really small. A microwave that triggered a hurricane. I blew. Hard and fast.

Ladies, this is not recommended behavior for anyone who wants a long-lasting marriage. Then we find out the author is seventy years old! And she admits that her husband is perfect in every way, and it's still not enough! It will never be enough for these crones.

> I am a grandmother. Yet in that roiling moment, screaming at my husband as if he represented every clueless male on the planet (and I every angry woman of 2018), I announced that I hate all men and wish all men were dead.

Does this not remind you of the blatant hatred and bigotry illustrated in Harper Lee's novel about Alabama in the thirties? It's as if the hard left feminists will never be satisfied until they get to line up and hurl rocks at all the men trying to just go to their jobs where they toil away cleaning sewage and rescuing trapped motorists and all the other things afforded to male privilege that women never want to do. It's like integration all over again. The left is back where they are most comfortable, persecuting people they hate. Honestly, what do women have to complain about in America in the Age of Information? I can't come up with a single valid thing. Rape? Rape is a crime! Sexual assault is a crime, and it is vigorously prosecuted. But here's a tip, ladies. If you are assaulted you better get yourself to a hospital immediately and get evidence. Then you call the police, right then *immediately*. You don't wait thirty years while all the evidence is cold and gone.

In Tom Robinson's case, the jury didn't care that there was no evidence against him and in fact the only two witnesses were shown to be inconsistent. Robinson was a black man and that was enough to render a guilty verdict for an Alabama jury. If we are not careful, the blatant bigotry of the feminist left against men is going to lead to the very same injustices that led to the deaths of so many innocent black man by lynching or execution. I have no doubt that many of the howling mobs of harpies want men like Kavanaugh dead. What makes them any different from the KKK? They use intimidation, threats and false charges against their perceived enemies. They go to their target's homes and try to break down doors. They run people out of establishments. There is a very short line to cross before someone gets hurt or killed and I suspect that's exactly what they want.

We must say no to The Mob and remember what our country believes about justice. Atticus Finch lays it out perfectly.

> But there is one way in this country in which all men are created equal--there is one human institution that makes a pauper the equal of a Rockefeller, the stupid man the equal of an Einstein, and the ignorant man the equal of any college president. That institution, gentlemen, is a court. It can be the Supreme Court of the United States or the humblest J.P. court in the land, or this honorable court which you serve. Our courts have their faults, as does any human institution, but in this country our courts are the great levelers, and in our courts all men are created equal.

And the reason the court is the best equalizer is because of the laws of due process which are supposed to be extended to every-one, not just a few. The presumption of innocence until proven guilty is absolutely sacred. Without it, we must submit to the mob and the mob's violent ignorance. They shot Tom Robinson. "Atticus had used every tool available to free men to save Tom Robinson, but in the secret courts of men's hearts Atticus has no case. Tom was a dead man the minute Mayella Ewell opened her mouth and screamed." Allowing more Dr. Fords to come forward against a man with no evidence and automatically give her an entitled ownership of "her truth" is to return to a time when a woman could open her mouth and condemn a man because of prevailing prejudice. *Hard pass.*

PART II

LYING

WRETCHES

 FROM THE 

MODERN

AGE

VICTORIA PRICE AND RUBY BATES

Never let it be said that America doesn't know what a lynch mob is. The very idea that we have talking heads on CNN, ABC, and even Fox News denying vociferously that any mob action is occurring (as we watch senators run out of restaurants and thugs take over Portland streets and beat up old people for trying to drive through their protests) is unbelievable. It makes me wonder if these news outlets have ever reviewed their own records written before 1960 or if they are just incredibly bad liars.

This country has a shameful history of injustice and mob action in the Jim Crow South. Lynch mobs were the favorite tool used against "uppity" blacks, or any black person on whom racists wanted to pin a crime. One particular story of the Scottsboro Boys stands out in history as one of the greatest injustices in America.

What went wrong in northern Alabama in 1931? Two wretched white women cried rape and nearly lied nine Negroes into the electric chair. Sure, they couldn't have done it if the jurors had not believed them. But once those poor white southerners heard two white women charge that black men had ravished them, they went out of their minds, lost what little self-control they had to begin with…"rape fantasies" often had "such irresistible verisimilitude that even the most experienced judges" were "misled in trials of innocent men accused of rape by hysterical women."[1]

Alabama in the 30's was a terrifying place for black Americans. Any black man accused of harming a white woman in any way would surely get death, whether through an unjust trial or through an illegal mob. It seems impossible that under those conditions any black man would get near a white woman for any reason unless they had a death wish. On top of the extreme racial segregation and prejudice, the Depression was in full swing and everyone was hungry and desperate, but no one more so than young black men.

The Scottsboro Boys were nine black boys, aged thirteen to nineteen, who were riding on top of a train to look for work. Any work they would be able to find would come to them last. Blacks were the last hired, and the first fired at the time. Some of them knew one another, others didn't. They got into a tussle with some white train hoppers, who the black boys ended up throwing off the train. None of them had any clue what the repercussions would be, or I'm sure they would have put up with the white boys' harassment. As they pulled into the next station, they were greeted by an armed posse waiting to take them to the sheriff. Unbeknownst to the boys, there were two white girls, Victoria Price and Ruby Bates, who had been traveling with the white boys who accused the black boys of gang rape out of meanness and spite.

Word had already spread in the small town of Scottsboro, and a mob had already formed. The Sheriff had to call in the National Guard to stop the mob from breaking down the jail door and murdering the boys. Anyone with experience in the American court system knows that court action takes years, if you're lucky, decades if you're not. But that's not how things worked in 1930's Alabama. They were tried and sentenced in *three days*.

> The boys were held without bail; local lawyers refused to defend them; local newspapers whipped up a mob spirit; and the judge scheduled the first trial for horse-swapping day, ensuring a tremendous crowd: ten thousand people, most of them armed with rifles and revolvers, poured into a town of fifteen hundred. Sheriffs beat the boys in an effort to extract confessions, but . . . they did not confess . . . On the night of the first day of the trials, however, Clarence Norris was taken out of his cell, alone, threatened, and badly beaten. He turned state's evidence the next day.[2]

The girls who accused them were known prostitutes with sordid pasts. It is very likely that they saw their chance to be treated well by Alabama society, having spent their lives on the outside, living in the poorest of the poor black neighborhoods, outcasts to their own race. Before their allegations of rape, Price and Bates were considered trash. One of them had been arrested for hugging a black man in public. These girls were raised with the black community. They played with black children, drank with black friends, had sex with black boys, and yet they turned on the boys on the train for some crumbs from the racist hierarchy of Alabama. Nothing they had done previously was admissible. The jury was not allowed to hear that they were prostitutes. Their tales of violent rape were not backed up by any medical evidence except for both of them having sperm inside them (not unusual for whores).

Victoria Price was a camera hound. She loved the spotlight and during the trial she often brought down the house with her ribald sense of humor and jokes. While nine teenage boys were fighting for their lives, she was playing a one-woman show on the stand.

The case gained national attention and interested the Communist party whose legal defense came to the aid of the boys. However, as Communists often do, they ended up alienating most of the people who could have helped get the boys a fair trial. Instead of using the system, the Communists tried to wreck the system by threatening judges, staging violent protests and generally causing uproar. *They never learn.*

Had the Communists been honest, intelligent, and wise, [Walter] White [of the NAACP] suggested, they might have made great gains. But, he contended, they were not. They

turned Alabama officials against the defendants with their
hostile telegrams and alienated the growing body of liberal
white southerners. [They] attacked the [NAACP], breaking up
its meetings and insanely charging that the members were "'in
league with the lyncher-bosses of the South" and plotting to
"murder the Scottsboro martyrs."[3]

Geez! That sure sounds familiar. It is almost certain that the
Kavanaugh mob activists turned off many people who would
otherwise be on their side politically, but there's only so much
incivility Americans can stand. We are law-loving people. We
understand that the law is what stands between us and anarchy.
Why is it that Communists always think breaking windows and
hurting people is the best way to get justice? A better way to get
what you want is to get to the polls and vote for people who share
your views. When you lose you don't get to burn the place down,
you pick yourself up and try again next time.

The NAACP at the time was making good inroads through
the justice system, but the Scottsboro Boys, on the advice of their
parents, hired the Communists. It was a big mistake.

With the national attention, ACLU director Hollace Ransdell
decided to travel to Alabama from New York to find out what she
could about the case. Race relations in the North in comparison to
the South were night and day. Most white people in the North
had no concept of what life was like for black people in the deep
South. I remember my dad telling me that he took a train from
Chicago to Florida in 1954 and was shocked at how open the
racial prejudice was. Chicago was no model of racial harmony by

any means, but there was no forced segregation in the North. No one ever told him what it was like in the South, and, at fourteen, on his family vacation, he was confused and uncomfortable as black people stepped off the sidewalk to allow his family to pass by in small towns in Alabama and Georgia. He did not understand the signs telling black people to go around back to use the bathroom or buy food. While racism was certainly an issue in Chicago, the blatant hatred and unequal treatment of black Americans in the South was so shocking to a white boy from the North that he still remembers it to this day with disgust.

Ransdell was similarly aghast at what she witnessed in Alabama.

> "In three days time . . . eight Negro boys all under 21, four of them under 18 and two of them sixteen or under, were hurried through trials which conformed only in outward appearance to the letter of the law. These eight boys, little more than children surrounded entirely by white hatred and blind, venomous prejudice were sentenced to be killed in the electric chair at the earliest possible moment permitted by law. It is no exaggeration certainly to call this a legal lynching,"[4]

Ransdell's observations as an outsider were fascinating.

Ransdell found Scottsboro a charming southern village of two thousand, situated in the midst of pleasant rolling hills. The people seemed mild-mannered, with kind, easy faces, friendly to one another and to her. Until she began asking about the trials.

Then the pleasant faces stiffened, laughing mouths grew narrow and sinister, soft eyes became cold and hard. Gentle and compassionate people were suddenly 'transformed by blind, unreasoning antipathy so that their lips parted and their eyes glowed with lust for the blood of black children' who had done nothing to them, and may not have done anything to anyone. In those glowing eyes all Negroes were brutes, brutes who could be kept in their place, and away from white women, only by ruthless oppression.[5]

These observations ring true today in the faces of people who seem like normal, nice people, until they find out they're talking to a Republican! Just try and tell someone suffering from Trump Derangement Syndrome that you voted for the *bad orange man.* I don't recommend it. The mobs of screaming women outside the courthouse during the Kavanaugh hearings are just such people. They have allowed their hatred of President Trump to blind them totally to all rationality. Instead, they want to destroy any person even remotely connected to Trump, even though that person has done nothing to them. Brett Kavanaugh has not harmed any of those howling beasts. He has not laid one finger on them, and yet they screamed for his blood on the shoddy evidence of one woman with immense amounts of privilege.

Just like Price and Bates, no one cared what was in Dr. Ford's background. No one cared if she was lying or not. It was enough that she told them what they wanted to hear to get them the result that they wanted. It's not dissimilar at all from a 1930's racist Alabama sham court, only instead of race being the catalyst, it's a war between the sexes based on politics. If Kavanaugh had been a Democrat, the shouting gorgons wouldn't have been there (Bill Clinton and Ted "waitress sandwich" Kennedy could confirm this). But Republicans are *bad,* and Republican men especially are *bad* and worthy of any insult or punishment, whether deserved or not, that can be heaped on their heads.

Much like the racist whites in the South, the feminist left feels completely justified in their hatred for Republican men. They've decided that they are less than human and, as such, deserve any indignity imaginable. There is a feminist writer at the *New York Times* whose Twitter history is awash in the most disgusting, racist nonsense you ever heard (unless you happened to live in the deep South during segregation.) Sarah Jeong tweeted, "Dumbass fucking white people marking up the internet with their opinions like dogs pissing on fire hydrants." "#CancelWhitePeople," showed up in another one of her gross tweets along with a chart showing how a man's whiteness directly correlates to how awful he is. Three guesses which side of the Kavanaugh debate she's on! *The New York Times* failed to do anything about this racist, misandrist on their staff because this way of thinking is completely accepted these days. In fact, if you don't think white people, and men in particular, are less than human, *you're the weird one.*

Have they even considered how this appears to be marching very quickly back to 1931 Alabama? Lord save us, because there's no way I could handle living among such ignorance. Reading about it is hard enough. Why would anyone want to go back there?

The Scottsboro Boys never got justice. Haywood Patterson was sentenced to death three times at three different trials even though Ruby Bates came clean and confessed that it was all a lie. The wicked Price refused to tell the truth and sent all nine to prison. Patterson escaped prison in 1949 and was apprehended in Michigan where a moral Governor refused to extradite him back to the insane state of Alabama. He died serving a prison sentence for a bar fight not long after. Clarence Norris got a life sentence and was pardoned in 1976. Andrew Wright was sentenced to 99 years and was paroled in 1950. Charlie Weems was sentenced to 105 years and was paroled in 1943. Ozzie Powell got 20 years for assault and was paroled in 1946. The rest of the boys had the charges dropped in 1937 after spending 6 years in jail. All of these men had their lives stolen from them because of the forked tongues of lying women.

TAWANA BRAWLEY

hite women are not the sole perpetrators of false allegations. All women are capable of lying and ruining men's lives. Tawana Brawley was just such a girl. She went missing from her home in Wappingers Falls, NY on November 24, 1987. She was found on November 28, four days later, wrapped in a garbage bag, smeared in feces, her body covered in racial epithets. She appeared unresponsive and unconscious and was taken to a hospital, where a full examination and rape kit were administered. Her physical condition did not meet any assault or exposure to the elements as she claimed. She was also faking her unconsciousness which doctors figured out fairly quickly. She would change her story a few times from "rape" to other sexual abuse she told investigators happened while she was held in the woods for four days by six white men. One of them was a well-known prosecutor and another a police officer.

The community outrage grew to epic proportions. In an ironic twist, Bill Cosby offered $25,000 reward for any information on Brawley's rapists. One wonders which girl he was drugging and raping later that night.

Like Mayella Ewell, Brawley is somewhat of a pitiable subject because it is believed she originated her tale out of fear that her, reportedly abusive, parents would find out she had disobeyed them. As young as she was at the time, only fifteen, youth and ignorance played a very big part in her actions. Whether she acted alone or had help is unclear. To this day, she still maintains that she was gang raped by six white men although she refused to cooperate with a Grand Jury investigation that set out to prove the facts. She also was sued by at least one victim and was ordered to pay him restitution, very little of which she has actually paid.

There was no evidence that any crime had occurred, but the usual race hustlers, like Al Sharpton in particular, turned her tall tale into a national shame that caused racial upheaval and destroyed innocent men. The grand jury report issued in January of 1987 was a scathing contradiction of Brawley's account and an indictment of those who had used her for political gain. I believe if a fair investigation was ever done, there would be a similar result in the Kavanaugh v. Ford affair. Who doesn't want federal investigators crawling all over Dianne Feinstein's office to find out what she was really up to?

Robert Abrams, then Attorney General of New York, was appointed the Special Prosecutor by Governor Mario Cuomo. The report he issued after an exhaustive investigation that lasted eight months, took testimony from over 180 witnesses, and contained more than 250 exhibits for evidence exonerated the accused and showed Brawley to be a liar. Perhaps worse, Al Sharpton had accused the law enforcement agencies of partaking in a vast cover-up, including using the KKK and the Irish mafia. It was truly absurd and outrageous behavior. The *New York Times* did a great video on the case that is still on YouTube which shows video evidence of Sharpton just making stuff up out of thin air, including defaming a man who had committed suicide.[1] Dead men can't defend themselves, so his family had to bear not only the loss of their son but the shame of false accusations and national outrage. The Grand Jury report is worth reading to see the depths of the damage that one liar can unleash on the world.

After these months of investigation, the Grand Jury found no evidence that a crime had been committed against Tawana Brawley and returned no indictments. The Grand Jury did, however, approve a detailed and thorough Report concerning the allegations made by Ms. Brawley, her family and her advisors. Public release of this Report was authorized by State Supreme Court Justice Angelo J. Ingrassia.

At the time the time the Grand Jury Report was released, I expressed publicly my strong view that the advisors to Tawana Brawley--Reverend Al Sharpton and lawyers Alton H. Maddox, Jr., and C. Vernon Mason--had engaged in an utterly reckless, dishonest and destructive course of conduct. In particular, I found it appalling that members of the bar would behave in such an irresponsible fashion, and I chose to file disciplinary charges concerning Mr. Maddox and Mr. Mason with the appropriate Grievance Committees. In these letters, I outlined repeated instances where I believe the lawyers violated disciplinary rules governing the conduct of attorneys.

The behavior by Brawley's attorneys was so bad that Maddox and Mason were both sued successfully by one of the accused and had to pay thousands in damages. They also faced disciplinary actions by the New York State Bar Association. Maddox had his law license suspended, and Mason was disbarred. Sharpton was the only one who emerged somehow unscathed. His only defense is to say he believed her. Brawley continues to claim that the rape happened. Her background suggests that she was an abused child who suffered a great deal at the hands of her stepfather, according to the *New York Times*.

> Nine sources, including neighbors and police officials, told the grand jury of violent quarrels in the King-Brawley household, ... Glenda Brawley had beaten her daughter for running away and spending nights with boys, investigators were told. And there were numerous reports of fights specifically between Mr. King and Miss Brawley. When she was arrested on shoplifting charges the previous May, the police had to intervene to prevent Mr. King from beating her at a police station . . .The grand jury also heard testimony of strains between Miss Brawley and Mr. King. One witness said Mr. King "would watch her exercise" and talked about the girl "in a real sexual way," sometimes describing her as a "fine fox." Another witness said Miss Brawley referred to Mr. King as a "filthy pervert.'[2]

Brawley appeared to have spent those four missing days running from her abusive stepfather and squatting in an apartment that her family had been kicked out of for non-payment.

There were many indications that she had been in the apartment. An acid-washed denim jacket she had been wearing when she vanished was found inside in a washing machine; feces like those found on Miss Brawley were on the jacket. Residues of burned clothing, similar to the scorched jeans she was wearing when found, were also discovered in the apartment. One pink slip-on shoe she was wearing had "KKK" carved in the toe; a razor blade that could have been used to cut these initials was found in the apartment."[3]

There are many reasons why a woman might lie about sexual assault. Fear of sexual and physical abuse is certainly one of them. Brawley's story is tragic. One can't help but feel empathy for her pitiable condition in life. Worse, it seems the adults around her led her down a path that would destroy the lives of innocent people. More than one witness overheard Brawley's mother admit to lying about what happened to her. Mrs. Brawley even spent time in prison for refusing to testify before the grand jury.

Two psychologists informed the grand jury that certain facts of the case pointed to false allegations, among them the victims inability to remember details of the event. If that sounds familiar to you then you may remember Dr. Ford's testimony of the alleged assault where she could remember nothing except that she claims she had one beer. Elements of her story also changed several times including how many people were at the party. Sometimes it was four, then it was seven, and some number in between. Ford also claimed that she had put a second front door in her home because of her PTSD issues. Ford also claimed to have fought with her husband over installing a "second front door" in her home in 2012. This argument was so bad she had to tell her therapist about it, and during that counseling session she claims she told the therapist it was because of some trauma she suffered at the hands of a high school student who could one day be a Supreme Court justice. But records show that she had that door installed in 2008, and it is used as the primary entrance and exit of renters she has had since the remodel. How exactly is a second front door supposed to help your "claustrophobia" and PTSD if you can't access it without going through your renter's home? And why would you be arguing about it in marriage therapy four years after the door was installed? Dr. Ford's testimony raised far more questions than it answered much like Tawana Brawley's tale of woe.

All allegations with severe consequences to the accused should be properly vetted and not politicized. Ignoring red flags (like a failure to remember key details) does no one any good. In Brawley's case, she is a sympathetic girl, subjected to things no child should ever face, and one wonders if her actions stemmed from survival instinct. The true villains of this story were her mother, step-father, and the political hustlers who used her for their own gain.

Dr. Ford shares some of that pitiable nature with Brawley, although far less so as she is a grown woman who should know better. But if it's true that she requested her information be kept confidential and did not wish to go public with her allegations like she claimed then the hate-hustlers have done it again. If we ever find out who in Diane Feinstein's office leaked Dr. Ford's letter to the press they should face serious consequences for using a woman as a pawn to take down a political foe. I think Senator John Kennedy (R-La.) said it best during the confirmation hearings. "To the person who leaked Dr. Ford's letter, to the person who breached Dr. Ford's anonymity, and to the person who did not tell her she could have avoided this by testifying privately in her home in California, you know who you are. You should bow your head in shame, in my opinion, and you should hide your head in a bag every day for the rest of your natural life."[4]

CRYSTAL GAIL MANGUM

By the time Crystal Gail Mangum was finished with her lying spree, she had implicated 46 members of the Duke University lacrosse team in rape. Mangum had a long history of mental problems, depression, and according to her father, lying about rape. She worked as a stripper and "escort," which was probably closer to prostitution than dating.

The Duke lacrosse team were some of the most well-liked boys on the whole campus. They threw the best parties, including an infamous "Tailgate" where they worked late into the night before making a huge apparatus to contain foam bubbles three to four feet deep for party goers to play in. They were known as a group of fun guys who also helped out in the community and studied hard. The breathless reports of the keg parties they held or noise complaints they earned could be repeated at every college campus across the country. College kids love to party. While this may not be news to you, it was reported to such a hysterical degree that one would believe that the Duke boys invented the kegger.

At one of their parties off campus, they made the catastrophic decision to hire strippers to come dance. The real crime in all of this is how much they were willing to pay for the two ne'er-do-wells who showed up and barely delivered. Crystal Mangum and Kim "Nikki" Roberts charged $400 each for 2 hours. They ended up dancing an entire 4 minutes before the boys began to feel uncomfortable when Mangum appeared too drunk to know what she was doing. The boys began to ask for refunds and insulted them a bit, and that's when things took a weird turn. The girls barricaded themselves in the bathroom deciding what to do. Mangum wanted to stay and get more money from the team. Roberts wanted to leave. The boys eventually slid money under the door to get them to leave! This was clearly the worst strip show anyone has ever seen.

They did eventually leave, but not without Mangum causing a scene in the backyard, dropping her purse and wallet and phone while banging on the door to be let back in. The boys thought about calling the cops to remove her but decided their coach would surely find out and be angry. Instead, they waited until she quieted down and went to check on her where she appeared to have passed out. One of the boys helped her to Roberts's car, and the two girls drove away.

Roberts reported that she couldn't get Mangum out of the car, and she tried to push her out when Mangum started saying terrifying things. "And clear as a bell, it's the only thing I heard clear as a bell out of her was, she said—she pretty much had her head down, but she said plain as day, 'Go ahead, put marks on me. That's what I want. Go ahead.' This remark 'chilled me to the bone,'" [1]Roberts told Chris Cuomo in an interview. Mangum obviously planned to frame the boys for assault of some kind. Unfortunately, Roberts kept that piece of information to herself during the investigation.

Mangum ended up in the hospital where she was about to be committed for involuntary observation because of her bizarre behavior. It was there that her allegations of rape came out in inconsistent ways, always changing.

While being interviewed at Duke, "her story changed several times", Durham police officer Gwendolen Sutton reported. Mangum told Sutton that she "ended up in the bathroom with five guys who forced her to have intercourse and perform sexual acts" and "later stated that she was penetrated by all five." That Brett had penetrated her vagina with his hands and penis. Also that "Nikki" [Roberts] had stolen her money and cell phone. But when Sergeant Shelton questioned her, she said that after her performance "some of the guys from the party pulled her from the vehicle and groped her" but nobody "forced her to have sex." Shelton walked out to the parking lot and called in to the watch commander. The woman had recanted the rape allegation, he reported. Then he heard that she had told a doctor she had been raped. Shelton went back and asked Mangum again if she had or had not been raped. She said that she did not want to talk to him anymore, started crying, and said something about being dragged into a bathroom.[2]

Those inconsistencies alone should have been enough for police to throw out her report as false even without the medical report that found absolutely nothing wrong with her.

> Now Mangum seemed alert and responsive, not drunk or impaired. Her hysterical behavior and crying suggested that something might have happened to her. But the doctors and nurses were unanimous in finding no physical evidence of the attack described by Crystal—that is, a brutal assault by three, five, or twenty varsity athletes, lasting a half hour. No bruises. No bleeding. No vaginal or anal tearing. No grimacing, sweating, changes in vital signs, or other symptoms ordinarily associated with the serious pain of which she complained.[3]

She did manage to get a bunch of drugs for her "pain" though.

Leave it to a crazed feminist nurse with a B.A. in "women's studies" to jam up justice with a misguided #BelieveWomen mental tick. "Tara Levicy, the [Sexual Assault Nurse Examiner] was to play a little-known but critical role in bringing about the prosecution of the lacrosse players. A strong feminist who had [directed and produced a college production of] *The Vagina Monologues*...and who saw herself as an advocate for rape victims, Levicy was later to acknowledge that she had never doubted the truthfulness of a single rape accuser."[4] *Not even the big fat lying liars like Mangum!* This solidifies my belief that anyone who is associated with the *Vagina Monologues,* wears a vagina costume, pussy hat, or consumes foods made in the shape of vaginas, (*don't* Google vagina cookies) should automatically be disqualified from any position of importance. Their brains are simply broken after pretending to make vaginas talk night after night, so steeped in feminist baloney they can no longer understand reality. If you don't believe me, check out this vagina-obsessed mom who brought vagina cookies to her second-grader's class and expected the teacher to use them to teach seven-year olds about vaginas as reported by the *Huffington Post.*

> [A] teacher describes how a mother brought cookies decorated to look like vaginas into her second grade class and said, "I decided you can use these to teach the kids about the woman's vagina today." When the teacher saw the assortment of frosted vaginas and realized this was no joke, she told the mother she could not serve the cookies because they were inappropriate. The mother flew into a rage, screaming that the teacher should be proud of her vagina. The poor teacher just stood there: "Utterly bemused and frozen from shock all I can do is stand and stare at the woman as the word 'vagina' is yelled in front of my second grade class about 987,000 times."[5]

These unhinged people do not need jobs in professions that could send anyone to jail. They should be roundly mocked and only employable in factories or morgues where they cannot have any interaction with the public. The Duke nurse was just such a person: stone-cold nuts.

Over the subsequent ten months, Levicy would repeatedly tell police that she thought Mangum had been raped, adjusting her theories to bat aside new evidence that the charge was false. Levicy later said that she had never seen a sexual assault victim behave hysterically in the way that Mangum did at Duke Hospital that night but dismissed the comparison as insignificant, since "no two sexual assault victims behave the same way." Shrugging off the absence of physical evidence of sexual assault, she would also explain away the lack of lacrosse-player DNA in Crystal with a feminist slogan: "Rape is about power, not passion." Dr. Anne Burgess, a pioneer in treatment of rape victims, would later tell defense attorneys that Levicy's analysis was fatally flawed. But for [District Attorney, Michael] Nifong, Levicy was an ideal witness.[6]

Any witness who would completely lie in order to stick to their preconceived notions of guilt would be ideal for a highly political District Attorney who was up for reelection and wanted to make a big splash in the news.

Michael Nifong disgraced the profession of attorney. Many people hate attorneys and tell dumb jokes about them, but person-ally, I've never known better, smarter people in all my life. My attorneys over the years have been some of the best people I've ever known who have moved mountains to get me justice. Great attorneys are next to firemen in importance, in my opinion, and should be revered. A Bar Association calendar probably wouldn't sell as well, but a good attorney is priceless. A bad attorney, on the other hand, is about two steps lower than demons sent out from

Satan himself to wreak havoc on the world and devour souls. A bad attorney can destroy lives. Mike Nifong was just such an attorney. I wouldn't be surprised if he smelled like sulfur when he belched.

"The prosecutor has more control over life, liberty and reputation than any other person in America. His discretion is tremendous. He can have citizens investigated, and, if he is that kind of person, he can have this done to the tune of public statements and veiled or unveiled intimations," said Robert H. Jackson, then the U.S. attorney general. His words remain a dire warning and accurate prediction about the conduct of Durham County, N.C., District Attorney Michael B. Nifong in prosecuting the Duke University lacrosse players. "In recent weeks, Mr. Nifong has admitted that he failed, as required, to turn potentially exculpatory information over to the defense: test results that showed the presence of semen from several other men, but not the Duke players, in swabs taken from the woman's body and clothing. Mr. Nifong says it was an accidental oversight. Yet the director of the DNA laboratory says that he and the prosecutor agreed to leave that information out of his report because it was so 'explosive.'"[7] The withholding of exculpatory evidence would get Nifong disbarred.

Other notable injustices in the case was Duke's insistence that the boys not tell their parents or lawyers when they were accused of this horrific crime. As a parent that burns me. These boys were allowed to be interrogated by police, who were clearly determined to pin the crime on them, with no lawyer. That is a disgusting violation of their constitutional rights. If you teach your kids only one thing, teach them to never speak to police without a lawyer, *ever*. "Evans, Flannery, and Zash did not invoke their constitutional rights. They answered every question. They wrote and signed detailed statements. They voluntarily gave DNA, blood, and hair samples, knowing that if any of their DNA were found in or on Mangum it would mean decades in prison."[8]

This is the worst thing anyone accused of any crime could do to themselves. Advisors kept telling the boys that if they hired a lawyer, the police would take that as an admission of guilt. *Huh?* That's absurd. The police were already operating from the presumption that the accused were guilty! A lawyer protects the rights of the accused. There is no possible way not having a lawyer would work out better for anyone facing criminal charges. If you are ever accused of a crime, do not speak to anyone, do not pass GO, do not collect $200, *go directly to a phone and call your lawyer.* (If you're like me, you have several on speed dial.)

The media, in their usual coordinated way, tried and convicted the lacrosse players by manipulating public opinion and refusing to print any other account but that of the accuser and Nifong. They focused on white boys "of privilege" and stoked racial hatred by repeating the lies that Mangum told about the boys hurling racial slurs at her. One of the worst was *New York Times* sports writer Selena Roberts.

At the intersection of entitlement and enablement, there is Duke University, virtuous on the outside, debauched on the inside. The season is over, but the paradox lives on in Duke's lacrosse team, a group of privileged players of fine pedigree entangled in a night that threatens to belie their standing as human beings...For days, Durham, North Carolina, residents and Duke students have rallied on behalf of sexual assault victims, hoping to stir more action out of Duke's president, Richard Brodhead. Does Brodhead dare to confront the culture behind the team's code of silence or would he fear being ridiculed as a snitch?[9]

Of course, the only reason the public was outraged to the point of rallying and protesting the university was because the fake news had whipped them up into unfounded rage by refusing to publish the inconsistencies in Mangum's story.

Where have we seen this before? Did MSNBC ever breathlessly report the fact that none of Dr. Ford's witnesses backed her up? Did CNN report that Dr. Ford lied in front of the senate committee when she claimed she has a fear of flying and then in the same breath was revealed as a world traveler? No one has heard any of those things unless they read the conservative press. The left-wing media plays a huge part in manipulating the public to fake outrage, which is why President Trump coined the term "fake news." They are total phonies. They know what they are leaving out is every bit as damning to Democrats as Nifong's DNA bombshell was to the Duke case. But they do it anyway hoping to snow you one more time and deliver those votes for their preferred party. It's an epic scam on the American people and justice.

It wasn't just the media who were to blame for the destruction of due process in this case, but the professorial staff at Duke as well. Known as the "Hateful 88," eighty-eight Duke professors went on the record in the newspaper in favor of skipping all that tiresome due process nonsense and getting right to the lynching of the three boys eventually charged. It was downright infuriating. John Podhoretz at the *New York Post* tore them a new one because, even after the boys were shown to be innocent, these mad professors continued to claim that there was a rape crisis on the Duke campus and so what they did was justified.

> At a contentious meeting on campus a few weeks after the accusation surfaced, Duke President Richard Brodhead said that it was important to wait until all the evidence was in before passing any sort of judgment. This was not acceptable to the 88 profs. "We're turning up the volume in a moment when some of the most vulnerable among us are being asked to quiet down while we wait," their letter said. "To the students speaking individually and to the protesters making collective noise, thank you for not waiting and for making yourselves heard."[10]

Thank you for not waiting? It's funny how these professors decided that waiting for facts and evidence to come out was not a worthwhile cause. This was certainly the same scenario during the Kavangaugh hearings when students and professors at Harvard agitated to remove Kavanaugh from his teaching position on campus before any evidence was presented. They succeeded.

Podhoretz continued, "So, at a moment when Duke students were being shadowed by a rape accusation, one-ninth of their professoriate had effectively declared that those students did not deserve the presumption of innocence – primarily because so many of their fellow students were supposedly being victimized by the atmosphere of 'racism and sexism.'"

This is what Social Justice Warriors (SJW) do when they are caught perpetrating a hoax. They claim that the seriousness of the charge still makes it all worthwhile because someone somewhere suffered rape making the persecution of a few white boys of "privilege" justifiable payback. Who cares if the boys' lives are upended and their families bankrupted by legal fees? Who cares if good names are ruined, lives are destroyed and our system of justice is corrupted? Feminist goals are achieved and that's all that matters!

The saying, "Better ten guilty men go free than one innocent man suffer" is a quote often attributed to many people, among them Sir William Blackstone, Benjamin Franklin, and Voltaire. But whoever said it, it's essential to the American system of justice. This sentiment used to be considered "liberal" and embraced by the left. No more. The current philosophy choking out reasonable objections screams the opposite. It's time to reverse the trend.

KERRI DUNN

Speaking of idiot professors, Kerri Dunn should go down in history as one of the worst campus employees *ever*. I reported on Dunn in David Horowitz's *News-RealBlog* in 2010.[1] "Kerri Dunn gave a barn-burner speech at Claremont College in California about racial discrimination and hatred. After her speech, she went to her car where she found it had been spray painted and vandalized with the words "kike whore" and "n***er lover." She immediately went back to the event and reported she was a victim of a hate crime. The school shut down classes for an entire day. The president of the college Pamela Gann released a statement.

Students and others responded spontaneously and forcefully last evening. They justifiably want Wednesday to be a day to gather to respond to this event and earlier events at The Claremont

Colleges. The students have organized numerous events throughout the day on Wednesday, including a sit-in on the North Quadrangle, and a 5-College rally on the CMC campus at 8:00 PM Wednesday night. In light of these events, I have also directed that CMC cancel classes today, and the other Claremont Colleges have also cancelled classes. One never lightly cancels classes, for to do so in some way suggests that we can be bullied by the perpetrators of such a heinous crime. Yet, we need every single person in this community to come together, to follow his or her conscience, and to start a process of regaining control of our community. In this way, we can hope to tell the perpetrators that they will in the end be defeated and repudiated.

The haters of hate had a big rally and just when everyone was whipped up into a racially fueled frenzy, two eyewitnesses came forward to report that Dunn had done the damage herself. (Cue leaking balloon sound effect.) Adding to her long history of criminal activity (shoplifting, driving on a fake license, theft . . .) she was convicted of two felony counts of attempted insurance fraud and one misdemeanor count of filing a false police report. The college then went on to "defeat and repudiate" the offender by suspending her with pay and renting her a replacement car. The president of a Scripps College wrote this missive when informed of the hoax illustrating why leftists should not be allowed in education.

Above all, we must focus on this: even if the vandalized car and slogans were a hoax, our responses last week were right and appropriate — in our community meeting March 10 in Balch Auditorium and in our strong participation in the evening rally at CMC with all The Claremont Colleges. However painful and confusing this latest development is, we cannot forget the reasons we were outraged in the first place; we cannot avoid the challenges that hatred poses to our community, to our country. We will continue to work to make our campuses welcoming, open, diverse, and productive so that all of us can freely teach and learn to the best of our abilities.

Would you be surprised to find out that Dunn is still a professor? Currently poisoning the minds of criminal justice students at John Jay School of Criminal Justice, Dunn is an adjunct professor of psychology. It's good she can diagnose her own mental problems, but it is rather puzzling how a person with her record can be instructing students in criminal justice. Dunn never saw a day in jail for her crimes. The police at the time said she could face penalties for lying to federal officers, but nothing came of it. Not like Paul Manafort, who has been put in solitary confinement for no good reason while his trial about tax evasion or something minor drags on. It's interesting how being a leftist seems to make one immune to criminal punishments. Faking a hate crime that could have sparked violent protests seems a lot more dangerous to me than moving money around in unconventional ways, but what do I know? Lock up the money launderers and let the psychos who vandalize their own cars walk among us. *I feel much safer.*

This is much like how I feel knowing that Christine Ford is

allowed to just go back to her life after destroying the reputation of someone without any evidence. She could have just made it all up, and we would never know. Someone needs to sue her. Justice will never be served if that woman, and the other two who came forward with bogus stories, aren't sued into oblivion for defamation. But much like Dunn, I doubt anything will ever happen to her, and she'll be allowed to live out the rest of her life as if she didn't do the most horrific thing any woman can do to a man, in public, and without remorse.

DR. LYNNE SNOWDEN

*P*rofessor Mike Adams is one of the funniest, smartest men I have ever met. He is a controversial professor of criminal justice at University of North Carolina Wilmington (UNCW) who also writes columns at *Townhall* that drive his leftist students and faculty crazy with rage. Adams made sure he got tenure before he came out of the conservative closet, however, and so, try as they might, they can't get rid of him.

My first face-to-face with Adams was at an event I helped set up at Monmouth College for him to speak to the College Republicans in 2005. I was into helping the youth back then, and I thought I'd used my writing contacts to spread the conservative message on college campuses. I couldn't think of a better guy to give that message than Adams. He had written a book called *Welcome To The Ivory Tower of Babel; Confessions of a Conservative College Professor*[1] that was a scathing rebuke of toxic, far-left campus atmosphere that was (and still is) actively at war with free speech. His entire talk was about the left's refusal to engage with ideas, instead using tactics to shut down any dissenting speech.

Shortly into his speech, a professor in the back of the room stood up and began filibustering him with silly, never-ending questions. He tried to answer her, but she wouldn't stop talking. He wrote a column about it later with a full transcript that she had no idea we would have because I was sitting in the audience recording. Good times.

> Professor Farhat Haq decided to shout me down from the back of the auditorium instead of hurling a key lime from the front row. Fortunately for me, Professor Farhat Haq (sounds like Far-left Crock) was sitting near a digital tape recorder when she launched into her tirade. I had the tape transcribed by a seasoned professional (read: fellow member of the vast right-wing conspiracy). The transcript does not adequately capture the shouting and singing (yes, singing) of Dr. Haq as she tried to disrupt an otherwise calm event.[2]

Haq went on and on trying to shout him down, sometimes singing, and basically making a fool out of herself. She later went on to give some of the students involved low grades in retaliation for hosting him. So you can imagine how popular Adams is on his campus with the women's studies professors and grievance mongers. He is a man with a target on his back.

In his book, Adams tells the tale of Dr. Lynn Snowden, whose actions could make her the leading psycho in a Stephen King novel. Snowden, a professor of terrorism, provided a list of offenses she claimed to have suffered to the university that included the "mutilation of a watch band" in her office, "destruction of tenure documents," and "tampering with computer including erasing bookmarks," among other things. The trouble began with her accusing another staff member, Cecil Willis, of "hate crimes" and "sexual harassment," neither of which ever proved to be true. In a letter to superiors at UNCW, Adams wrote,

Dear Mr. White: As you know, last November an officer of the UNCW police department asked me to stop by the station to discuss a matter involving former Faculty Senate President Lynne Snowden. When I arrived at the police station, the officer informed me that Snowden had reported to them that her office was being burglarized. She claimed that the burglar was spraying some form of poison in the office in an apparent act of 'workplace terrorism.' As you may know, Snowden has written a book on terrorism and teaches a course on the subject. I was quite pleased with the professionalism of the officer who interviewed me in November. He immediately expressed the view that Snowden was in need of a psychiatrist. That was a relief to hear since she had named me as the person responsible for the 'terrorism' of her office. As you already know, she also accused our department chair, Cecil Willis, of using his master keys to let me into her office to spray the mysterious toxins that she claimed were cutting off the circulation in her legs. I found it particularly interesting that Snowden told the officer that her doctors were not able to find anything physically wrong with her. I was also interested to find that Snowden convinced an adjunct faculty member and a criminal justice major to come into her office to 'swatch' her desk in order to preserve a sample of this mysterious poison gas. The officer also said that Snowden suspected that the mysterious toxin was tear gas . . . After Christmas break I noticed that Snowden's ability to function in the workplace was diminished. On many occasions I saw her wearing slippers as she walked into class, dragging her left leg behind her. That tear gas must have been pretty strong to cut off the circulation in her left leg. However, I did wonder why it didn't affect the 80-pound Labrador retriever that she took into her office at night for personal protection. Of course, I also wondered what kind of education the students were getting in Snowden's classes. By March of this year, I noticed that Snowden had stopped going into her office altogether. She began using the computer in the main office and started advising students in the computer lab just down the hall. It was also becoming common knowledge on campus that Snowden believed that terrorists were after her. A colleague of mine saw her one evening around six o'clock in the office hallway, using a towel to get the mail out of her mailbox before dropping it into a plastic bag. According to another colleague, she was afraid to touch it until she had sanitized it in a microwave oven . . . The university's refusal to deal with this dangerous faculty member shows just how morally depraved this institution has become. If Snowden really believes her bizarre allegations, she is mentally unfit to teach at the university. If, on the other hand, she does not believe the allegations, she is morally unfit to teach at the university."[3]

Snowden was never reprimanded for her false accusations and remains a professor at UNCW. It took six months for Adams to be cleared of poisoning her. It is clear none of what Snowden alleged was true, but it is not clear if Snowden was trying to cause trouble for Adams or if she's just stone-cold crazy. What is certain is the parents paying big money to UNCW are being ripped off with staff like her teaching their kids. A quick perusal of Rate My Professor came up with 43 reviews, most of which sounded like this, "Dr. Snowden has been THE worst professor I've ever had at UNCW. I took her class online. And before the semester even started she sent out an email asking us not to email her because she has 'other important classes on campus.'" Others called her "extremely disorganized," "confusing," and "not entirely there."

It's no laughing matter what this woman attempted to do to two men she works with. It's terrifying to me that anyone would choose to #BelieveWomen like this. Snowden is unhinged, unstable, and probably in need of heavy medication. She's living in some sort of state of paranoia which is unhealthy and dangerous for others around her. It makes me wonder if she has a second front door.

EMMA SULKOWICZ "MATTRESS GIRL"

Emma Sulkowicz should go down in history as one of the most despicable women on the planet. You may remember this shameless hussy from her infamous mattress protest at Columbia University where she hauled a mattress around campus all day to protest the University not expelling another student she claimed raped her.

While Sulkowicz earned fame and accolades from some of the highest personages in the United States and was invited to the State of the Union by Senator Kristen Gilllibrand, the student she falsely accused, Paul Nungesser, led a life of public shame and institutionalized oppression. The *New York Times* compared Sulkowicz to Jesus. Yes, *that Jesus*.

You can, for the moment, call Emma Sulkowicz a typically messianic artist, and she won't object. I used the phrase, sitting in her tiny studio at Columbia University on Thursday, as we discussed "Carry That Weight." This is the succinct and powerful performance piece that is her senior art thesis as well as her protest against sexual assault on campus, especially the one she says she endured.

"Carry that Weight," which is beginning its fourth week, involves Ms. Sulkowicz carrying a 50-pound mattress wherever she goes on campus (but not off campus). Analogies to the Stations of the Cross may come to mind, especially when friends or strangers spontaneously step forward and help her carry her burden, which is both actual and symbolic. Of course another analogy is to Hester Prynne and her scarlet letter, albeit an extra heavy version that Ms. Sulkowicz has taken up by choice, to call attention to her plight and the plight of other women who feel university officials have failed to deter or adequately punish such assaults. The carried mattress also implies disruption and uprootedness, which call to mind refugees or homeless people.[1]

The fawning doesn't end there. The slavering article continues, masking activism as journalism.

"Carry That Weight" might be called an artwork of last resort. It is the culmination of two years of pain, humiliation, frustration and righteous anger that began in 2012. On the evening of the first day of classes of her sophomore year, Ms. Sulkowicz said, she was anally raped in her dorm room by a fellow student with whom she had had consensual sex twice before, according to the police report.

In the aftermath, Ms. Sulkowicz suffered in silence, then filed a complaint with the university. This led to a hearing before a panel that found him not responsible, according to a campus newspaper report in The Columbia Spectator, a decision that was upheld upon appeal. After that disappointment, she said, a trip last May to file a report with the police was so upsetting she didn't follow through, although she secretly recorded it on her cellphone.

There is no mention of any pain or humiliation that her victim suffered. For that you have to go to the *National Review,* which covered this story in a much more professional way than the *New York Times,* which later had to admit the story was "messy."[2]Mona Charen, however, painted a much more accurate portrayal of the effect of Sulkowicz's lies on the life of Nungesser in an article in The National Review called "It's High Time Columbia's Matress Girl Was Discredited," writing,

Sulkowicz filed charges with the university and the New York police. (She later alleged that the New York police mistreated her.) Both investigated. Both declined to take action against him. It was then that Sulkowicz undertook her mattress performance as an attempt to brand Nungesser a rapist and drive him from Columbia. He was shunned and anathematized. As Cathy Young reported in Reason magazine, Sulkowicz launched a full-on harassment campaign.

In the summer of 2014, other students and a professor pressured Nungesser to drop out of a scholarship-paid class trip to Russia, Mongolia, and China. That October, on a "Day of Action'"against sexual assault, several mattress-toting activists showed up in one of his classes, where they stared at him and took his picture. Keyboard warriors in the social media urged making his life "a living hell" and sometimes called for violent retaliation.

Nungesser finished his degree, but he also supplied evidence to Young that undermines the case against him — evidence that was not even admitted to the tribunal that cleared him. Nungesser produced Facebook messages the two exchanged within 48 hours of the alleged rape.[3]

The Facebook messages were hardly indicative of anyone who had suffered violent rape. Nungesser had her on record asking to see him and telling him she loved him after the alleged "rape." No charges were ever brought against him but that did not stop the university from continuing to allow him to be discriminated against and harassed. *The Daily Beast* got the story directly from Nungesser a mere two years after he was dragged through the press.

Even before the investigation began, the charge had immediate consequences. Nungesser was placed on restricted access to university buildings other than his own dorm; these "interim measures" made it extremely difficult to continue in his campus job as an audiovisual technician (especially since he was not allowed to explain why he was under these restrictions) and to attend the counseling sessions he had started. Meanwhile, it became obvious that despite confidentiality rules, news of the accusation was spreading: Within a few days, Nungesser says he was being conspicuously shunned by many fellow students.[4]

After Nungesser was exonerated by the school investigation (and Title IX kangaroo court) the mattress show began. *The Daily Beast* expose continued.

Sulkowicz's act, which is also her senior project for her visual arts degree, has been praised as both protest and art. To Nungesser, however, it is something else altogether: harassment. "It's explicitly designed to bully me into leaving the school—she has said so repeatedly," he says, referring to Sulkowicz's statement that she will carry the mattress until either Nungesser leaves Columbia or they both graduate. "That is not art. If she was doing this for artistic self-expression, or exploration of her identity—all these are valid motives. Scaring another student into leaving university is not a valid motive." Nungesser also says he has been the target of social-media threats. A Tumblr post that began to circulate last September said, "The name of Emma Sulkowicz's rapist is Jean-Paul Nungesser. Don't let him have any feeling of anonymity or security. Rapists don't get the luxury of feeling comfortable." Around the same time, Nungesser says that he and his parents spotted and eventually removed a Facebook post that had a far more ominous tone, stating, "I'm only pissed that I'm not in NY to CUT HIS THROAT MYSELF!"

Nungesser finally sued the University and won an undisclosed settlement. The University only made the following statement.

[A]fter the conclusion of the [sexual misconduct] investigation, Paul's remaining time at Columbia became very difficult for him and not what Columbia would want any of its students to experience. . . . Columbia will continue to review and update its policies toward ensuring that every student — accuser and accused, including those like Paul who are found not responsible — is treated respectfully and as a full member of the Columbia community."[5]

Sulkowicz never dropped the mattress act and even took it onstage with her for graduation. This woman is shameless. Going on to prove everyone right in labeling her an attention whore (along with literal whore) Sulkowicz made a career out of "performance art" where she degraded herself in public with more and more bizarre and perverted acts. *The National Review* reported her metamorphisis from "mattress girl" to whatever this is. "Seeking to keep her notoriety alive, she has created a 'performance art' piece in which she is tied up in her scanties, hoisted in the air, and beaten for the amusement and edification of spectators."[6] But that's not all. When the news articles died down about her after the trussed up beatings she promptly released a sex tape where she reenacts that violent "rape" she claims suffered in college. Milo Yiannopoulos describes it better than I ever could. He's just so deliciously mean.[7]

Good porn never starts with a pop quiz so we're off to a poor start with the site's bizarre and incomprehensible statements which reach for, but fail to grasp, profundity. Sulkowicz's inner nine-year-old is never far from the surface: questions she asks visitors include "Do you think I'm the perfect victim or the world's worst victim?" and "Do you hate me? If so, how does it feel to hate me?"

And then it's down to business. . .Porn star Mercedes Carrera described it earlier today as "a bad amateur sex tape from an attention-seeking histrionic." She was being too generous... but let's plough on.

At the start of the tape, Sulkowicz enters a dorm room, blue-haired — for that is the uniform of the Internet feminist and masturbatory social justice warrior — pursued by a bear. Online critics have expressed dismay at the fact she hasn't bothered to make the carpet match the drapes by dying her pubic hair blue. It's a recent innovation known to the social justice community as "the full San Francisco." Perhaps this fashion-forward intimate grooming trend is yet to appear on the east coast.

What follows is punchy. By which I mean Sulkowicz gets punched, though she insists in the unhinged copy on her website that everything in the video is consensual. There follows much quivering of flesh and a deeply unsatisfactory blow job. As a queer, I can tell you it is probably the most lazily and messily administered head I have seen in years. If this is the sort of oral sex straight men are getting, can anyone blame them for retreating into pornography and video games?

Perhaps worse than subpar fellatio is the next section of the video where Sulkowicz acts out the "violent" portion of the "rape" not very convincingly. Milo continues,

If you know what hentai is, you'll be familiar with the spectacle of a blue-haired Asian woman screaming for it all to stop whilst not really meaning it with a man pounding away noiselessly like a mechanistic rape engine. It's not exactly an original set-up.

Perhaps the most despicable section of the film is the creepily self-conscious fetal position into which Sulkowicz places herself after her sexual partner has left the room, clothes in hand. She's practised that for hours, has our girl. For how long, one wonders, did she rehearse?

One suspects years.

It's telling, I think, that in Sulkowicz's purported college dorm room there are no books. She has the same lack of interest in aesthetics as she does in intellectual enrichment: both in her choice of sexual partner (apparently satisfactory member notwithstanding) and the grim, bare walls with which she surrounds herself. Though I expect the austerity of her room reflects her barren emotional interior really rather well.

You can tell "dad bods" are in fashion because both of the people in this video have one. But you do at least have to give an actress credit for doing nude scenes with a man who has larger breasts than she does. Sulkowicz's size queendom apparently extends to love handles and leave the viewer sympathetic to the travails of her infamous mattress.

It's revealing of her vanity that she insists on being filmed from four angles. Every crevasse of her unappealing naked body must be considered. Her congressional interlocutor is a gruesome sight in three dimensions, chosen, probably, to make young Emma look thinner. Which doesn't work, I'm sorry to say.

All in all, it's a tawdry, miserable encounter that tells us nothing about sexual assault or sex itself but quite a bit about the quasi-demonic inner workings of one Emma Sulkowicz.

And these are the women for whom the left roll out the red carpet —lying whores. Sulkowicz has a bright future ahead of her as long as she continues her "art" which she appears eager to do. Expect more self-debasement from her in the future and none of it interesting or honest.

DINA MACKNEY

People use family court and divorces to destroy their former lovers all the time. Both sexes are guilty of it but women seem to have the upper hand in custody cases. In one particularly egregious case, Christopher Mackney wrote in his suicide note that Dina Mackney, her father, and the courts drove him to his final act. After trying desperately to take control of his blog, so the world would never hear his story, Dina failed, and his suicide note was published for all the world to read. It led to a book by journalist Michael Volpe called "Bullied to Death, Chris Mackney's Kafkaesque Divorce."[1] In his last attempt to get justice, Mackney wrote as a desperate man.

I never wanted to speak out about any of this. All I wanted was a fair and reasonable child support, fair and reasonable visitation with my children and be free to move on with my life. The only reason I chose to write a blog and speak out about the abuse was because I thought it would give me some kind of leverage, as I had none.

I made it clear to my ex- wife's attorney that the family court was not allowing me to change the orders, I had no information about my children and my child support was far beyond my ability to pay.

I was hoping for some act of good faith to let me know that they wanted to reduce the conflict. It never came, not in 5 years. I felt that my only recourse was to speak out about the abuse and injustice in order to get the legal and psychological help I needed to manage the conflict, so that we could both parent our children. I reached out to my ex- wife's attorney again to ask for ANY other alternative. . .When I read online about the patterns of behavior of high conflict divorce and how my ex-wife was the one blocking access to the children and negatively interpreting everything I did, I spoke out and tried to address the source of conflict. No one would tell me I was wrong, but no one would speak out about the abuse on my behalf, not the Doctors or attorneys. Experts in psychology have called it abuse, but none would make such a 'diagnosis', which I could then take to Court to obtain relief. As long as the pattern of behavior was not called 'abuse', my reactions would not be viewed in its proper context by the Court.

The way I looked at it was that if I remained silent, the abuse would continue. It did. When I finally decided to speak out, they didn't care.

They didn't care about how it would affect Dr. Samenow, Judge Bellows, our children, themselves or anyone else. They were not going to take their foot off the back of my neck. They were fully invested in having me out of my children's lives, permanently. Bullying and parental alienation are all forms of emotional abuse. Psychopathy is an emotional dysfunction. People with psychopathy are identified by how they handle conflict. It is the disturbing lack of empathy, guilt shame, remorse that give them away. They are completely unaffected by the distress of others. As long as they get what they want, you may never see that side of them. . .I had never been arrested, depressed, homeless or suicidal before this family court process. The stress and pressure applied to me was deliberate and nothing I could do or say would get me any relief. Nothing I or my attorneys said to my ex- wife's attorney or to the Court made any difference. Truth, facts, evidence or even the best interest of my children had no affect on the outcome. The family court system is broken. . .I took my own life because I had come to the conclusion that there was nothing I could do or say to end the abuse. Every time I got up off my knees, I would get knocked back down. They were not going to let me be the father I wanted to be to my children. People may think I am a coward for giving up on my children, but I didn't see how I was going to heal from this. I have no money for an attorney, therapy or medication. I have lost 4 jobs because of this process. I was going to be at their mercy for the rest of my life and they had shown me none. Being alienated, legally abused, emotionally abused, isolated and financially ruined are all a recipe for suicide. I wish I were stronger to keep going, but the emotional pain and fear of going to court and jail became overwhelming. I became paralyzed with fear.

I couldn't flee and I could not fight. I was never going to be allowed to heal or recover. I wish I were better at articulating the psychological and emotional trauma I experienced. I could fill a book with all the lies and mysterious rulings of the Court. Never have I experienced this kind of pain. I asked for help, but good men did nothing and evil prevailed. All I wanted was a Guardian Ad Litem for my children. Any third party would have been easily been able to confirm or refute all of my allegations, which is why none was ever appointed to protect the children or reduce the conflict.

Abuse is about power and control. Stand up for the abused and speak out. If someone speaks out about abuse, believe them. Please teach my children empathy and about emotional invalidation and 'gas – lighting' or they may end up like me. God have mercy on my soul.[2]

After writing this last entry, Chris Mackney got into his car and put a hole in his head with a shotgun. This was a man, who many described as a good father, utterly destroyed by a vindictive woman and a broken court system. There is no justification for any of this. Tens of thousands of parents are going through it right now in family courts where the so-called "silver bullet" technique is employed to alienate them from their children and benefit the opposing spouse. This technique utilizes false claims of abuse and orders of protection to establish that your opponent is a bad person and therefore not able to be a good parent. This kind of dishonest abuse of the system should not be allowed, but for the moment it is put into practice daily to destroy more people like Chris Mackney for no good reason.

KHADIJA ALTAMIMI & YASMIN SEWEID

In the wake of the 2016 presidential election, there seemed to be a rash of "hate crimes" against minorities. It seemed that way because the *New York Times*, the *Washington Post* and all the alphabet channels ran with ridiculous tall tales of such night after night. We were told that Trump supporters across the nation were emboldened to harm minorities after Trump's election, and they did so with gusto, ripping off hijabs, attacking people with racial slurs, and more. The only problem was, none of it was true.

Ann Coulter wrote an article published on Breitbart— "The Great Hijab Cover-Up"—that detailed many of the hoaxes.

I've read through dozens of SPLC 'hate crimes' and they are all lies. The Muslim girls in particular seem to be very spirited liars.

Since the election, there have been vivid stories from across the nation of Trump supporters tearing off Muslim girls' hijabs —at the University of Michigan (since retracted), Louisiana State University (also retracted), San Diego State University (that too was retracted), the New York City subway (again: retracted), and the University of New Mexico (no witnesses, won't reveal attacker's name or report the incident for investigation).

The main take-away from all these stories is: We sure have taken in a lot of Muslims! They seem to have trouble assimilating to American laws about not committing mass murder, but the good news is, when it comes to America's culture of victimhood, they assimilate like fish to water!...At this point, any claim of 'hate' directed at Muslims, blacks, gays or Hispanics by Trump supporters should be treated as if it's a UFO sighting: presumed false, unless documented with irrefutable evidence.But until the NPLC is up and running, here are some tips for journalists:

— Real hate crimes do not begin with laughably implausible scenarios. Try to use a modicum of common sense.

— They are almost always captured on videotape or at least are seen by actual witnesses who give statements to the police. Lachrymose accounts posted on Facebook do not constitute evidence.

— They generally result in medical treatment and arrests."[1]

This would have been helpful in the reporting of the alleged "hate crime" reported by Khadija Altamimi on the University of

Louisiana campus along with a spate of other campus reports in November of 2016. Here were some of the headlines:

- "Hate Crimes Spike in Wake of Donald Trump's Win with 897 Reports Recorded in 10 Days," *The Independent.*
- "Woman in Hijab Attacked at UL-Lafayette by Man in Trump Hat" *Nola*
- "Muslim Women Wearing Hijabs Assaulted Just Hours After Trump's Win" *NBC News*
- "Muslim Students at Two Colleges Report Violent Assaults By Donald Trump Supporters," *Seventeen*
- "University of Michigan student wearing a hijab was threatened with being set on fire, police say," *Washington Post*
- "Wearing Hijab in Trump's America," *CNN*
- "Drunk men screaming Trump's name try to rip off Muslim student's hijab as straphangers stand idly by on East Side subway, cops say," *New York Daily News*

Every single one of the articles claiming assaults had to be updated with new information that the girls had made it all up, but not before the fake news generated protests and fear all over the country that minorities were being targeted by Trump supporters. This led to more actual violence against Trump supporters at rallies where they were egged on film, battered, bloodied, and hospitalized by Antifa and others who thought they were "punching Nazis." And honestly, why wouldn't they? Respected news organizations told them that Trump supporters were beating up minorities! Nevermind that none of that was true, people believe the first story they read. They do not go back weeks later to see a small correction or update at the bottom of the article that says, "Sorry, we were wrong and she lied." Fake news is the enemy of the people because it creates violent situations and divisions that should never have occurred if they weren't actively trying to fit stories into their biases. None of the reporters involved waited for due process. None of them waited for investigations. Instead, they reported the accusations as true. This is not journalism.

On November 11, 2016, Khadija Altamimi went to police and reported that she had been attacked. The Lafayette police wrote her account in their report #16-00364659.

> Ms. Altamimi stated that as she was walking on Smith Street, a silver/gray sedan traveling North on Smith Street passed her up and then turned in front of her and parked. Two white males then exited the vehicle and began to walk towards her. Ms. Altamimi stated one white male is described as wearing a red Donald Trump 'Make America Great Again' hat, with long dirty blonde hair, wearing a gray shirt and gray sweatpants. 2nd Suspect is described as having dark hair with a scruffy beard, and also wearing gray sweatpants."

That description alone should have set off lots of alarm bells considering she described cartoon characters that sound more like

Joe Dirt than real people. The "victim" continued to describe her violent assault at the hands of these dastardly men.

> As the males exited the vehicle and started walking towards her, they started yelling at Ms. Altamini stating 'What's up girl? Where are you going? You don't belong here!' Ms. Altamimi stated she got scared and turned around and started walking away ... At this time, both suspects approached the victim from behind and struck the victim in the back with what the victim believes was an unknown metal object. One suspect began to pull her hair and grab her hijab and pulled her to the ground. Once on the ground, Ms. Altamimi stated she was on her stomach while both suspects began to punch her in the back with closed fist. Ms. Altamimi stated they yelled, 'You terrorist bitch!' several times at her while punching her in the back. Ms. Altamimi stated the suspect stole her black hijab and her pink NY and Company wallet ... Ms. Altamimi showed me the grey hoodie which she had on that had two holes in the back side where the suspects had either hit or grabbed her causing it to rip ... Ms. Altamimi stated she sustained minor injuries to her upper and lower back but refused medical attention by Acadian Ambulance.

Well, isn't that convenient? She reported getting beaten with closed fists by two men and refused medical treatment? The only explanation for that is because she did not want medical professionals to reveal that there was no evidence of the alleged attack. It is a mystery why the police would allow a victim to deny medical attention when the victim is asking them to put someone in jail for a crime. Don't you have to have evidence of the crime in order to do that? However, Lafayette police did a thorough investigation and found her story to be full of holes. The detective assigned to the case met with Altamimi on November 9 where she claimed she could not give clothing descriptions because she was on her face at the time of the attack. Unfortunately, she had already described her attackers in detail on the 6th. The detective wrote in his report, "I noted no obvious signs of injury on Ms. Altamimi. She claimed she was struck in the head and face but no bruising, swelling, or redness was observed." Witnesses reported seeing her and remembering her looking fine, not disheveled and not upset in any way after the alleged incident. The detective continued, "It should also be noted that where Ms. Altamimi was indicating [that where] the incident occured, the CC's Coffee house, has outside seating which is typically full of students during class hours. This outside seating has a clear view down Smith Street. There were no witnesses that observed this incident." When police asked her to come in for a recorded statement on the record, they got to the truth.

> Ms. Altamimi eventually stated she fabricated the entire incident. She stated she was in the building of Maxim Doucet where she observed a white male wearing a Trump Hat, who called her a terrorist. Ms. Altamimi stated she then fabricated the incident because she was hurt by the statement. She made this same statement to an agent with the Federal Bureau of Investigation who was present for the interview due to the

possibility of her initial complaint being a hate crime. Ms. Altamimi advised she fabricated the story due to her father catching her not wearing her head scarf and she needed a reason why. Ms. Altamimi indicated she no longer wishes to be a Muslim but does not know how to tell her father. This incident has been revised to criminal mischief and is cleared by the arrest of Ms. Altamimi.

Her conflicting statements during her recant tell the real story. There was no man in a MAGA hat, or if there was he certainly didn't speak to her. This girl was looking for a way out of an abusive situation with her uber-religious father. It had nothing to do with Trump's election. But according to the press, the election of Trump turned the entire country into racist, xeno-phobic, assaulters. This is why, when Trump says fake news is the enemy of the people, he is 100% right. Look at how the *New York Daily News* reported another hoax by another lying lunatic, Yasmin Seweid.[2] "Straphangers stood by and watched as three drunk white men repeatedly screamed 'Donald Trump!' and hurled anti-Islam slurs Thursday at a Muslim Baruch College student before trying to rip her hijab off of her head on an East Side subway, the woman told the *Daily News*." This supposedly happened on a subway full of people, and no one had video of this event? The *New York Daily News* never bothered to find some of these alleged witnesses. They just printed it as if it were true.

It turned out that Seweid also lied to avoid harsh punishment for missing curfew by her Muslim father.[3] Perhaps what we should learn from these events is that Muslim women have much more to fear from Muslim men than from Trump supporters. The *New York Daily News* was forced to report the truth with Seweid being arrested for making a false police report. "'Her strict Muslim parents allegedly forced Seweid to shave her head over the incident and were upset that she was dating a Christian,' sources said. The bareheaded Baruch College student, not wearing her hijab, was charged with filing a false report and released after her arraignment early Thursday in Manhattan Criminal Court." It's a strange choice that they used the word "allegedly" to describe the state of Seweid's hair which was obvious from the photographs that it was completely shaved off. Their use of the the word is meant to protect Seweid's abusive Muslim parents from suspicion, while they did not use the word "allegedly" in regards to Seweid's claim of assault.

Luckily, there were no named men in any of these assaults but there were innocent people dragged through the mud and defamed: Trump supporters. And that was no mistake but a willful hit job carried out by fake news to harm the president and his supporters with lies and fabrications to further the narrative that Trump supporters are violent and dangerous people. The perpetrators themselves were also harmed by the fake news media. If the media had waited for investigations they would never have reported these stories nationally (if at all), and the girls who were suffering abuse at home would not have had to go through the national shaming on top of it. In an effort to defame Trump and his supporters, the fake news media threw abuse victims under their destruction bus and then backed up over them.

UNIDENTIFIED LIAR IN NEW YORK

In 1991, a woman ran to a parked police car in hysterics claiming she had been kidnapped and raped by three men. 19-year-old Gregory Counts and 21-year-old Van Dyke Perry were arrested and charged with rape, sodomy, kidnapping, and more. The third man was never caught. The prosecution had a very weak case with no physical evidence. They relied solely on the testimony of the accuser, which wasn't always consistent. Physical evidence proved the semen recovered from the accuser did not match either of the defendants. A jury convicted them anyway. In May of 2018, Perry and Counts were exonerated when the Innocence Project got involved, and their accuser admitted she lied. To this day, her name has not been released under a New York statute that says victims of rape cannot be identified. VanDyke Perry and Gregory Counts were wrongfully imprisoned for a combined 37 years on the word of a lying woman.

"[T]he woman at the center of it all admitted in April that she had lied. Perry and Counts were convicted solely on her testimony. 'She admitted she fabricated her account,' Manhattan District Attorney Cyrus R. Vance, Jr. said of the unnamed woman."[1] But according Vance, there was nothing he could do to bring the accuser to justice because the statute of limitations had run out.

At the very least, the public should know her identity, but the state of New York refuses to identify her. I sent a FOIA request, which was eventually denied on appeal. The following was sent to me by the Office of the Deputy Commissioner of the New York Police Department.

> The appeal is denied because, absent a notarized authorization from the victim, the records requested are specifically exempted from disclosure by state or federal statute . . . Civil Rights Law Section 50-b prohibits the disclosure of records that tend to identify the victim of a sex offense. Specifically, subdivision (1) of §50(b) states that: 'the identity of any victim of a sex offense, as defined in article one hundred thirty or §255.25 of the penal law, shall be confidential. No report, paper, picture, photograph, court file, or other documents, in the custody or possession of any public officer or employee, which identifies such victim shall be made available for public inspection. No such public officer or employee shall disclose any portion of any police report, court file, or other document which tends to

identify such a victim except as provided in subdivision two of this section.' **The outcome of the prosecution of the criminal case is not a determinative factor in whether §50-b applies. Consequently, the Freedom of Information Law provides no rights of access to those records,** *regardless of the outcome of the criminal matter.*

Unbelievably, the state says that the outcome of a case doesn't matter! So if a "victim" of a rape turns out to be the perpetrator of a fraud, nothing happens to her! I also asked for any documents showing police had charged her with filing a false police report but received nothing in return. Very few people who make false allegations ever face any consequences that would make the next person think twice before trying it.

Elizabeth Coast accused her neighbor of sexually assaulting her when her parents caught her watching porn. The neighbor boy did four years hard time before she decided to confess that she lied. Her punishment was two months in jail served only on weekends.[2] Breana Harmon got no jail time in Texas for falsely claiming that she was raped by three black men. While there were no men arrested for the hoax, it stirred up racial hatred which can have serious consequences.[3] In Christine Blasey-Ford's case, she got a million dollars for her efforts to destroy Justice Kavanaugh! Sources say she's busy planning more renovation on her house, perhaps a third front door to go with the second front door she claims her alleged encounter with Brett Kavanaugh inspired her to install.

Julie Swetnick, the woman who accused Kavanaugh of facilitating gang rapes and drugging girls, has also not faced any consequence nor been charged with lying under oath even though she admitted that what she claimed happened in her sworn statement did not happen.

In the sworn statement, Swetnick said, "I also witnessed efforts by Mark Judge, Brett Kavanaugh, and others to cause girls to become inebriated and disoriented so they could then be 'gang raped' in a side room or bedroom by a 'train' of numerous boys. I have a firm recollection of seeing boys lined up outside rooms at many of these parties waiting for their 'turn' with a girl inside the room. These boys included Mark Judge and Brett Kavanaugh." Then she was interviewed by NBC News and she contradicted her own statement. Instead of saying she saw lines, she then said she saw them "huddled" by doors but didn't know what was going on inside the rooms. She also changed her story on her allegation that Kavanaugh was spiking the punch with drugs. "I became aware of efforts by Mark Judge, Brett Kavanaugh, and others to 'spike' the punch at the house parties I attended," is what she said in her written statement. When questioned by NBC, the story changed. So she went from claiming he facilitated the drugging of women to "he handed out red cups and I don't know what he did." *Lock her up.*

Based on other cases similar to this one, absolutely nothing will happen to her except she might get a book deal and a million dollars in GoFundMe campaigns.

Smarmy lawyers cooking up damsels in distress to hurt famous people is an old trick that should never be allowed in our justice system. Any lawyer who finds women (and often pays them) to accuse a public figure should lose his or her law license. Alan Dershowitz, constitutional lawyer, was also falsely accused of sexual misconduct with a minor by disreputable lawyers. He wrote an article in the *Wall Street Journal* in 2012 about his harrowing experience.

> I now stand accused of crimes I did not commit, by an unnamed woman whom I don't know and never met. I am also being sued for defaming my accusers. I still have no opportunity to respond in court to the false charges, though I am now seeking to intervene in the lawsuit in which the accusation was filed. I have submitted a sworn statement denying the accusations with great specificity. The court has not yet decided whether to accept my motion.
>
> I feel like a victim of a drive-by shooting or the object of scribbled graffiti on the wall of a bathroom stall. I may never have the opportunity to prove my innocence, or to have my accusers prove the false charges, in any court of law. But because I am relatively well known—a double-edge sword in these situations—I can at least fight back in the court of public opinion, though at the very high cost—in legal fees, loss of insurance coverage and the possibility of a large monetary judgment against me. Imagine the same thing happening to a person who did not have the resources to fight back.
>
> There is a gaping hole in our legal system that allows lawyers to bring irrelevant accusations against innocent nonparties in court papers that insulate them from any

consequences, and to deny the falsely accused any opportunity to respond.

The law must be changed to shatter this hall of mirrors I face and others might. There must be consequences for those who file accusations with no offer to prove them and no legal responsibility if they are categorically—and disprovably—false."[4]

Dershowitz didn't get justice until 2016 when the lawyers involved admitted they made a "mistake," and they withdrew the false claims.

Every single time an election is upon us, Gloria Allred and her dead-eyed spawn, Lisa Bloom (and more recently Creepy Porn Lawyer, Michael Avenatti), appear with some woman to accuse the Republican in the election of groping or other sexul misconduct. They offer no proof, just allegation and insinuation. And every time this happens, Democrats want us to believe it's true while the media reports it as fact at the bidding of their Democrat overlords. The Allred demons have done this to Herman Cain (can't have an uppity black man rise too high in the Republican party), Bill O'Reilly, and Donald Trump. She found four women to climb out from under rocks to accuse Trump of stupid things like *he invited me to dinner and tried to kiss me.* In every case, the women's stories amounted to nothing but failed come-ons, each one admitting that they were able to walk away without Trump stopping them. Some predator! I don't think any of them were telling the truth. In Summer Zervos's case, her own family came out to the press to say she's a habitual liar and dying for attention. Lisa Bloom also represented Kathy Griffin when she made the terrible life choice to "behead" the president for a photoshoot, and, strangely, Bloom also took known woman-abuser Harvey Weinstein on as a client for a short time.

It was funny to watch her expose her partisan beliefs so clearly by taking him on as a client. It seems Bloom only cares about "victims" of Republicans. If a Democrat does the victimizing, one of the Allred bloodsuckers are happy to help. The appearance of the Allred twins during tense political battles is something that can be counted on like the rising of the sun (or Broward County finding an extra hundred thousand ballots several days after any election that will ensure a win for Democrats). I think it's a sure bet that Creepy Porn Lawyer Michael Avenatti was going to be a part of this demonic duo doing his part to bring Republicans down with horse-faced women, until he was charged with domestic violence and crawled back under the rock from which he came. I feel certain he will resurface at some point.

What's also certain is that none of the women who come forward with false allegations will be punished in any way even if they are proven liars. Instead, they go on to write books, raise money on false pretenses, or go on stripping tours to "Make America Horny Again," like Stormy Daniels, the porn star accuser of Trump's, actually did.

WANETTA GIBSON

Brian Banks was a rising football star at age seventeen when his life was abruptly flushed down the toilet by a double-crossing tramp. Banks had been on his way to the high school guidance counselor's office to talk about college when he bumped into Wanetta Gibson and took a detour with her under a stairwell for a little kissing. According to Gibson, he dragged her under the stairs and raped her. Despite no physical evidence of rape, Bank's lawyer advised him to plead "no contest," probably because the lawyer was lazy and didn't want to do any real work. Banks expected to get no more than 18 months but caught a judge in a bad mood who sentenced him to six years.

Banks had always dreamed of being in the NFL. After his sentencing and false imprisonment, he never gave up on his dream and continued to train. He served all six years. Meanwhile, Gibson sued the school district for her "rape" and won a 1.5

million-dollar settlement. Fortunately for Banks, she was dumb enough to friend him on Facebook after he got out of prison and admitted to lying. He got her on camera confessing that she lied, but she would not agree to tell the prosecutor for fear of losing her payout. After showing that recording to prosecutors, Banks was exonerated.

Unlike most other falsely accused men, Banks' story has a happy ending. In 2013, Banks was signed with the Atlanta Falcons, and his dream of playing in the NFL came true. He only got to play in four games before being released, but he was then hired by the NFL to work in their Department of Operations.

Around the same time, the school district sued Gibson and won a 2.6 million-dollar judgment. It's one of the rare examples when justice stepped in and won the day. If only all lying vixens faced the same sort of consequences.

TAYLIER TIBBETS

Taylier Tibbets is the perfect example of why men should always think first before blindly trusting women. Tibbets got angry with the father of her son, so she accused him of child abuse. She went so far as to doctor photographs of their son to make him appear bruised and injured.

Like most tale-spinning hellions, Tibbets opened a GoFundMe account to raise money on the defamation of her victim. His reputation was destroyed. When she was finally caught in her lies, she received a slap on the wrist in the form of a $350 fine and 30 days in jail. Explanations for why her sentence was so light ranged from "she's so young" to "she had no criminal record." Men don't seem to get those considerations when they are sentenced. For some reason, women who lie and ruin lives seem to have privilege in the justice system and get off easy.

Meanwhile, Tibbets' victim suffered untold embarrassment,

shame, lost jobs, and loss of reputation that he will never recover. Family court is full of stories of men falsely accused by their ex-wives and former girlfriends of committing horrific crimes against children so they can win custody.

In another egregious case, Darryl Ginyard got what very few men in his situation ever see: an $852,000 judgment against his ex-wife and full custody of his children, after it was proven she lied about him sexually abusing them. Ginyard suffered parental alienation as a result of her lies and damage to his reputation. Judgments like this are rare. Most of the time, women get away with it, leading their victims to lives of sorrow and sometimes suicide.

A man known only as Jeremy A. left a suicide note for his family after being the victim of false abuse allegations by his ex-wife. It read, "FAMILY LAW NEEDS REFORM. I recommend mandated lower costs and less reward for false claims of abuse. Parental Alienation is devastating. I loved my children as much as a husband and father could. I see no light. Recommend; an authority consistent during high conflict separations: It is exploited in family law. Sorry Dad and Angie. I'm very sorry."[1]

Jay Cheshire of Southampton, England was 17 when he was falsely accused of rape. The accusation and investigation that followed so traumatized him that even after the charges were dropped, Cheshire committed suicide. To add calamity to tragedy, Jay's mother committed suicide one year after her son. A false allegation by one villainous harridan took two lives. The accuser was never even identified let alone punished as she should have been for manslaughter.

Where are the #MeToo warriors who care when innocent people are driven to suicide by vindictive, wicked women and unjust courts? It's simply not fashionable to stand up for men these days and so we all ignore their pain. Women are marching and demanding rights they already have while wrenching basic human rights away from men for revenge and self-interest. Women like this are disgusting and make me ashamed to share chromosomes with them. They have assured that I will never #BelieveWomen without hard evidence.

SEXUAL HARASSMENT GOES
BOTH WAYS

*I*f you followed the #MeToo explosion on social media, you would believe that only men are capable of harassing women, but that is provably false. *Psychology Today* reported recently that men suffer silently from sexual harassment at work.

"According to a recent survey, about one-third of all working men reported at least one form of sexual harassment in the previous year. Of the 7,809 sexual harassment charges filed in 2011 with the U.S. Equal Employment Opportunity Commision (EEOC), 16.1 percent were filed by men. By 2013, this had risen to 17.6 percent."[1]

Men widely report their personal stories of harassment on Reddit and other social media but the general consensus is that nothing can be done, but, if the situation was reversed, it would probably end in jail time for the man. Here are a sampling of stories shared on Reddit as reported in the *UK Guardian.*[2]

"When I was an IT intern at 22, I worked with a middle aged woman who would constantly harass me. 'If I was fixing her computer, she'd say stuff like 'while you're down there...' She would do this at company outings too, and it made me incredibly uncomfortable." Another victim told a similarly shocking tale. "I was on my knees fixing a door handle. Some of the women walked by and said, 'That's where men need to be.' I did nothing, but I knew had the situation been reversed, I would have lost my job."

Male servers at bars and restaurants also face regular sexual harassment, and no one seems to care much. One waiter reported that a woman patron groped him. "She ran up to me as I was collecting glasses and shoved her hand down my trousers. She also had very long and very sharp nails. I remember her screaming 'But you're a man!' when I told her to leave the building before I called the police. The rest of the party turned on me and called me every homophobic name under the sun and left." A bartender reported being groped by another employee, a female waitress. "[I] was at a bar in New Orleans a few months ago when a waitress randomly grabbed my D (over the pants) because she 'wanted to know what I was working with.'"

These types of events are unconscionable, but no one is marching and yelling for the right of men not to be abused by women in the workplace. If anything, women have the view that a man should feel flattered if he is treated like this, or even worse, that it is somehow payback for the inequality women have faced.

Stereotypes enforced by media haven't helped. The popular character of Samantha in "Sex and the City" sexually harassed every man she ever met including uninvited touching and unsolicited sex talk. Instead of ever facing rejection or push back, these men were depicted as lapping up this overt sexual attention. Samantha was the epitome of the feminist idea of the empowered sexual woman who could act like a man, even as she embodied the men feminists claim to despise; the gropers, the wolf-whistlers and the dirty-talkers.

The concept of men being sexually harassed is almost a joke. Women laugh about it regularly because the "power disparity" involved. Many women think that because men are physically more powerful, it means they cannot be harassed by a woman. This is false. A perfect example is the shocking past life of Donna Hylton, embraced by the feminists of the Women's March as a leader and speaker. (These women don't always protest, but when they do, a Republican is the target. None of them ever marched in opposition to the horrendous sexual deviance of Bill Clinton who actually did grab a pussy in the White House, that wasn't his wife's, belonging to a young intern, and was credibly accused of rape along with indecent exposure and harassment of several women. The very concerned women have never marched against him because he has the right letter behind his name.)

But this gaggle of women who claim to have the moral high ground on sexual ethics hired Donna Hylton to give a speech at their rally. Shortly after, *The American Spectator* exposed Hylton's sordid past. She had been a part of a gang that had kidnapped a man and held him for twenty days while sexually abusing and torturing him until he died. "For the next 15 to 20 days (police aren't sure just when Vigliarole died), the man was starved, burned, beaten, and tortured."[3] The torture included starving, beating, crushing his testicles and shoving a metal rod up his anus.

In the modern womyn's movement, men don't rate. Hylton's victim was not a concern for the Women's March organizers. They saw Hylton as a victim because she has reinvented herself as an activist for women in prison and an advocate for women of color. Either nobody bothered to ask why she was in prison or nobody cared that it was for the rape, torture, and murder of a man.

Hylton spoke passionately at the Women's March saying "This is about women in this country who refuse to be marginalized, sexualized, and abused, and silenced...I'm here to tell you today that we are human! We are women and we count." Hylton did not mention the man she dehumanized for twenty days and eventually murdered. He apparently doesn't count.

#METOO HYPOCRITES

It isn't surprising that the Women's March that claims to be about equality embraces psychopaths, and Donna Hylton wasn't the only one! Linda Sarsour, famed Sharia apologist and anti-semite, is one of the most public faces of the Women's March. Sarsour famously took to Twitter and claimed, "There is NOT ONE example of Muslims trying to impose Sharia on anyone. No legislations. Anti-Muslim rallies playing on the gullible." Perhaps there are no legislations (although I doubt it) but there are plenty of examples of Muslims imposing Sharia law on a populace by force.

The most obvious example is the Taliban's reign of terror in Afghanistan. Under strict Sharia law, women in Afghanistan could not go outside without a full burqa or without a male relative, were forced into marriages, were not allowed to speak loudly in public, banned from wearing high heels, banned on television and radio, banned from employment, not allowed on buses with men, kept out of schools, and confined in apartments with the windows painted black. (That's an abbreviated list of horrors. There are many more.) And who could forget the soccer stadiums turned into killing fields where women were shot in the head for small rebellions like wearing nail polish. Not only is life for women terrible under Sharia, but LGBTQ is an acronym that carries a death sentence. American Muslims like to claim that Islam is pro-gay, but any country where Sharia is the law is a country that kills and tortures homosexuals. There are currently seventy-three countries where homosexuality is outlawed, a vast majority of them are countries with Muslim majorities and some form of Sharia law.

These are the horrors that American leftists overlook in their zealous rush to be "inclusive" of Muslims like Sarsour. Allowing that woman to be the face of the American women's movement would turn out to be the greatest mistake the pussy-hat marchers made (next to those awful hats). It's unfortunate that her extreme support of Sharia, responsible for the oppression and abuse of millions of women, wasn't the scandal to bring her down. It should have been the obvious fly in the ointment, but because the American left is desperate for Islam to actually be the peaceful religion they imagine, they ignore its many atrocities worldwide. In the end, it was Sarsour's deep hatred for Jews that did her in.

In 2019, the movement fizzled when Jewish women's groups pulled out of the Women's March because of the leaders' obvious anti-semitism and cozy relationship with Jew-hater Louis Farrakahn.

The anti-semitism that Vanessa Wruble, a Jewish woman, faced while trying to be a part of the march she helped build is shocking. *The New York Times* told the story.[1]

Within days of Donald J. Trump's election, a diverse group of women united by their concern about the incoming administration gathered at a restaurant in New York to plan a protest march in Washington. They had seen the idea floating on Facebook and wanted to turn it into a reality. The unity did not last long. Vanessa Wruble, a Brooklyn-based activist, said she told the group that her Jewish heritage inspired her to try to help repair the world. But she said the conversation took a turn when Tamika Mallory, a black gun control activist, and Carmen Perez, a Latina criminal justice reform activist, replied that Jews needed to confront their own role in racism.

The insults got worse and worse. According to Wruble, she was regularly lectured about the evil Jews and was kept out of any role of significance.

At that first meeting, Ms. Wruble said, they seemed to want to educate her about a dark side of Jewish history, and told her that Jewish people played a large role in the slave trade and the prison industry. "I was taken aback," said Ms. Wruble in her first extensive interview about her experience organizing the

Women's March. "I thought, 'Maybe there are things I don't know about my own people.'" She said she went home that night and searched Google to read about the Jewish role in the slave trade. Up popped a review of "The Secret Relationship Between Blacks and the Jews," a 1991 book by Mr. Farrakhan, which asserts that Jews were especially culpable. Henry Louis Gates Jr., a Harvard professor, has called the book the "bible of the new anti-Semitism."

Behind the scenes, Ms. Wruble said she felt cast aside. She said she was told by one of the march leaders that "we really couldn't center Jewish women in this or we might turn off groups like Black Lives Matter." While Black Lives Matter is a diffuse movement, some activists have issued statements expressing solidarity with Palestinians under Israeli occupation. At one point, Ms. Wruble said she asked about security for the march and was told by the leaders that the Nation of Islam would be providing it. "I said, 'You are going to open up the march to intense criticism,'" Ms. Wruble said, warning that it would be a red flag for Jews. She said they dismissed her concerns in a heated email exchange and accused her of unfairly maligning the Nation of Islam.

In Wruble's final exchange with the Women's March leaders, the deep Jew-hatred came pouring out in a heated exchange that was witnessed by others.

Even though the march was a success, Ms. Wruble said that she felt angry and that the event's official leaders were more focused on celebrity than building the movement. She also felt they were unwilling to confront their own bias against Jews. At a meeting days after the march, an argument broke out between Ms. Wruble and the other leaders.

Ms. Mallory and Ms. Perez began berating Ms. Wruble, according to Evvie Harmon, a white woman who helped organize the march, and who attended the meeting at Ms. Mallory's apartment complex.

"They were talking about, 'You people this,' and 'You people that' and the kicker was, 'You people hold all the wealth.' I was like, 'Oh my God, they are talking about her being Jewish,'" said Ms. Harmon, whose account was first published by Tablet. "The greatest regret of my life was not standing up and saying 'This is wrong.'"

Even Alyssa Milano, that know-nothing former starlet, knew enough to back away from Sarsour. Shortly after Laura Loomer confronted her about Sarsour's blatant anti-woman and anti-semitic views, Milano backtracked on her support of the Women's March. In an interview with *The Advocate,* she disavowed Sarsour and other leaders who stood by Farrakahn. "Any time that there is any bigotry or anti-Semitism in that respect, it needs to be called out and addressed. I'm disappointed in the leadership of the Women's March that they haven't done it adequately."[2] Milano, a fixture in the Women's March from its inception did not appear at any events after that. The Women's

March is effectively dead because they were willing to embrace murderers, rapists, anti-semites, and homophobes who are "down for the cause" without noticing how hypocritical and stupid they look for screaming "racist homophobes" at conservative opponents.

THE COVINGTON CATHOLIC BOYS

If the mothers of America saw our husbands in Brett Kavanaugh, we saw our sons in the Covington Catholic boys. The boys from Covington Catholic High School made a catastrophic mistake in 2019 when they went on a pilgrimage from their home in Kentucky to our nation's capital to partake in the March for Life with thousands of other pro-life Americans. Their mistake was two-fold—attending a pro-life event and wearing MAGA hats while white and smiling. This set off a series of unfortunate events that can only be described as despicable where their lives were torn apart, turned upside down, and shaken by the rabid left. This isn't a specific incident where the lies of one woman destroyed a man but the lies of many women (and a few men) in the media conspired to lie about these teens and continue lying even when proven false to advance the narrative that "all Trump supporters are racist Nazis."

It began with a single fifty-four second video with no sound posted to Twitter by an anonymous user. This video appeared to show a group of MAGA hat-wearing boys taunting a Native American elder who was playing a drum. The text that went along with the video said, "MAGA wearing white boy mocking Uncle Nate as he plays his handrum...this shit got me so heated. Remember this little shits face and the countless youth who think just like this." Nathan Phillips, the Native American with the drum, went on every news channel imaginable and claimed the boys had surrounded him while he was minding his own business and began chanting "build the wall!" in his face. He claimed that he, a grown man, was intimidated by smiling fifteen year olds. That was the first of many versions of the same event he would tell.

The video clip went viral, and, in no time, major members of the press were denouncing the Covington boys in the strongest terms. Kathy Griffin called for them to be doxed (which means have their names and addresses posted online). She wanted to specifically "name and shame" them. S.E. Cupp, former conservative turned rabid left-winger, went on her show on CNN and excoriated the boys for "angrily chanting build the wall" at Native American "Vietnam veteran" Nathan Phillips. Newly elected congresswoman Ilhan Omar tweeted, "The boys were protesting a woman's right to choose & yelled 'it's not rape if you enjoy it'...were taunting 5 Black men before they surrounded Phillips and led racist chants." She later deleted that spurious allegation with no apology.

There is a long list of powerful women who jumped onto the

Covington hate-wagon including Andrea Mitchell, Alyssa Milano, Elizabeth Warren, Joy Reid, Savannah Guthrie, Maggie Haberman of the *New York Times*, and more. They whipped up a frenzy of hatred against the boys by spreading defamatory allegations that turned out to be totally false. The truth was that the boys were being insulted and attacked by black Hebrew Israelites including being called "crackers" and "incest babies" and "school shooters" while they stood there saying nothing waiting for their bus. On top of the abuse from the Hebrew Israelites, the Native American group led by Nathan Phillips walked into the crowd of boys banging a drum until choosing to stop in front of the now famous "smirking boy" Nick Sandmann. Sandmann's only crime was refusing to be intimidated by the activists. He never spoke a word and smiled in the face of rude adults hellbent on painting the him and his friends as racists.

Predictably, Conservative Inc., comprised of members of the old guard like Bill Kristol, Rich Lowry and his Never Trump army at the National Review, wrote scathing articles including one titled, "Covington Catholic kids might as well have spit on the cross." It was a shameful pile-on by people who should have known better than to trust the drive-by media. At least, the conservative press retracted and apologized. The same cannot be said for the members of the left-wing press and mainstream #FakeNews media who either deleted tweets with no apology or doubled down on false information.

By the time all the videos with the audio were discovered, the damage to the boys' reputations was already complete. The entire country was calling for the heads of the Covington Catholic

School boys. Not only did The Mob want them suspended from school, but many were contacting colleges asking them not to admit any Covington graduates. The diocese of Covington threw the kids under the bus immediately without getting the facts. The denouncement from the Church was swift and harsh. (Far swifter and harsher than any denouncement of sex offenders in the clergy.) The diocese even claimed it was considering expulsion. In what seemed like merely hours after the incident, the diocese released a strong condemnation of the boys.[1]

> We condemn the actions of the Covington Catholic High School students towards Nathan Phillips specifically, and Native Americans in general, Jan. 18, after the March for Life, in Washington, D.C.," the diocese's statement said. "We extend our deepest apologies to Mr. Phillips. This behavior is opposed to the Church's teachings on the dignity and respect of the human person. The matter is being investigated and we will take appropriate action, up to and including expulsion. We know this incident also has tainted the entire witness of the March for Life and express our most sincere apologies to all those who attended the March and all those who support the pro-life movement.

The bishop's immediate condemnation lent credibility to the allegations which gave the hate-mongers on Twitter more ammunition to go after the kids. And go after them they did. There were death threats, including one prominent Disney writer saying the children should be fed head first into a woodchipper accompanied by a graphic illustration showing blood on snow. He later said he was "joking."[2]

The families of the boys were immediately under siege. Internet sleuths uncovered many of the identities of the boys (including some students who weren't even there), and the death threats began in earnest. The Mob began calling the employers of the kids' parents trying to get them fired for having "racist" sons. Once The Mob gets ahold of a victim, it doesn't let go without total destruction. The fact that the boys were not the aggressors, nor did they chant "build the wall" did not deter The Mob. Video evidence of the boys being harassed by black protesters and video showing Nathan Phillips approaching the boys (which was the opposite of what he claimed) did not slow down the raging lunatics out to destroy the Catholic students. Several of the media personalities apologized and deleted their initial tweets because they realized that the reports were false, but it was too late to stop the narrative they created.

To this day, opinion is still split on this issue. Those on the right believe the boys. Those on the left believe the aggrieved Indian (even though evidence proves him a liar.) Phillips wasn't even a Vietnam vet. He was a mechanic in the marines who never left the continental United States but was seen in interviews claiming to be a "Vietnam vet" who got spit on when he "came home." The press ignored this case of stolen valor and claimed that they were the ones who messed up that reporting and that Phillips had never said he was a "Vietnam vet" but a "Vietnam era vet." This claim is false. There is video of Phillips claiming to have served in Vietnam.[3]

This is a pretty clear-cut case of defamation against the Covington Catholic boys all the way around. They were lied about, defamed, terrified, and persecuted for "thought crimes" they did not commit. Lawyers jumped on the chance to sue the big media companies and individuals that took part in it. Sandmann has a great lawyer who put together a damning video of the events as they occurred which should win them a big settlement in court.[4] It remains to be seen if the lawsuits will go forward and what the outcome will be, but hopefully it will mean humiliation and major damages for everyone involved in the smearing of innocent boys.

While there were men who participated in the disparaging of the boys, it appeared as if the women were leading the charge. Powerful women with big microphones amplified this hoax to huge audiences and made it the viral story that it was. Their lack of concern or sympathy for boys who could have been their sons was astounding. It's not something you expect women to take part in, the public dragging of minor children, but they did it with glee and signaled to everyone that these minors were fair game. It is yet one more example of how women are not better than men, are not morally or ethically superior, and when gathered into a mob can be vicious, unforgiving, and merciless. Even after all the facts emerged, many on the left still maintain the boys were at fault for wearing MAGA hats, not bowing and scraping in the face of minorities, and for being at a pro-life march in the first place! Aliza Worthington of *Crooks and Liars* wrote,

Lots of new video has emerged from varying angles and

perspectives, the longest being nearly 2 hours long. Upshot? White teenaged boys in MAGA hats are still bigoted, entitled little jerks...Ummmmmmmm...first of all, I can think of a few actions Nick Sandmann might have taken that would have been more respectful of others, and less likely to lead to conflict than the ones he and his friends took. The first one would have involved not attending the March For Life rally at all. But they did, so let's move on. The second would have been to not wear MAGA gear to announce that they STILL supported the Racist Sexual Assaulter-In-Chief in Office right now. The third would have been to back up, back his friends up, to give Nathan Phillips passage through without surrounding him, staring him in the face, while he placed his body between a group of white teenagers and the Black Hebrew Israelites to keep them apart.[5]

Attending a pro-life march is enough to rationalize the destruction of the futures of minors according to this nasty woman. Nevermind that polls show a majority of Americans favor major restrictions on abortion and at least half the country is staunchly pro-life. If your views don't align with the media-approved views, you shouldn't be allowed to march, or protest, or go to college, according to them. Also note how she continues to misreports facts that can be seen on video! Phillips did not "place his body between the teens and the protesters" like some savior. The boys did not surround him either. He could have walked around them and up the steps to the Lincoln Memorial at any time, but he did not do that. He came in agitating to stir up more insults, while his fellow Native Americans were telling the boys to "go back to Europe. This is not your land." That doesn't sound like peace-making to me.

Worthington's sentiments weren't unique. Many people blamed the hats as if the hats justified any action against the boys. Alyssa Milano doubled down and tweeted, "The MAGA hat is the new white hood."[6] Molly O'Reilly of Commonweal Magazine (a Catholic publication!) wrote "You don't let your kid wear a MAGA hat and then act offended when they get taken for a racist."[7] CNN published an op-ed by Isaac Bailey claiming that everyone who wears the MAGA hat is a racist. "The MAGA hat, like the Confederate flag, wouldn't elicit outraged reactions if it were only a piece of cloth that harkened back to bygone days never to be relived. But it isn't. It is a signifier for those who believe America was great during some point in the past they dare not name, knowing if they do, it would reveal a time when it was worse for people of color."[8] What rubbish.

I've had this argument with seemingly rational people who claim that wearing a "Make America Great Again" hat is looking for a fight. My response is always, "What kind of immature moron would start a fight over a hat?" The demonization of a political hat is the most bizarre thing about this whole era and will probably go down in history as the weirdest thing that sparked the next American Civil War. We're already being taxed at astronomical rates our forefathers killed people over, but the minute the left starts dictating to us what we can wear it might be the final straw. Is this really who we are; people too fragile to deal with a political slogan?

It's important to note that even after all the facts came out showing the Covington boys were the victims of hatred, bigotry and aggression, the left still continues to spin that it was their fault for wearing the hats. Ask any feminist, however, if it's a woman's fault for getting raped because she was dressed provocatively and be prepared to hear that clothes can never be the cause of an assault.

PART III

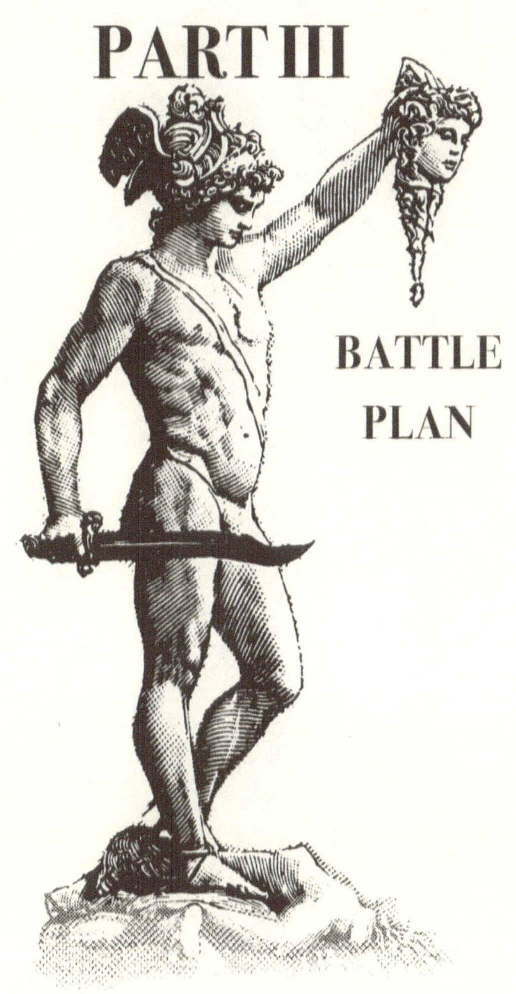

BATTLE

PLAN

HOW TO HARPYPROOF YOUR SON

I t's a testament to the absurd time in which we live when the following information will seem revolutionary, but that's exactly how it was received when I first wrote about it on *PJ Media.* It even got me invited onto the Tucker Carlson Show on Fox News. It seems that our collective consciousness is starving for common sense solutions to the absolute madhouse we find ourselves living in. Up is down, down is up; girls are boys, boys are girls; the guilty are innocent and the innocent guilty; and no one knows how to protect themselves from the ever-encroaching backwards philosophy being forced on us from every direction.

It's quite simple. Return to traditional Western values and save yourselves and your progeny from the madness. Raising children today is increasingly difficult, especially when it comes to sons. It's an anti-male world. How else to explain the absolute insanity of Title IX college rules that if a boy and a girl are both drunk and they have sex, she can't consent but he can? This ushered in a whole new wave of girls who were able to assuage their own guilty consciences for making bad decisions by crying rape in the morning.

In the light of these new rules, you need to arm your son with old rules to save him from false allegations.

TAKE HIM TO CHURCH

Church attendance is dwindling in America, especially among men. Everyone is too advanced for that old superstitious nonsense. But there is no arguing that studying the Ten Commandments and living them will keep a person out of a lot of trouble. It is imperative that young men grow up learning their worth and value and the worth and value of others. Solid biblical teaching does this quite well and has, for 2000 years, instilled a code of conduct in humanity that leads to peace and prosperity if followed. A study of black men found that church was a factor in lifting them out of poverty and installing them into the middle class. "Black men who frequently attended church services at a young age are also more likely to reach the middle class or higher when they are in their fifties: 53% of those men who attended church as young men made it, compared to 43% who did not."[1]

Men who attend church regularly also impart that good habit to their children. "A study by the Swiss government found that '. . . if a father does not go to church--no matter how faithful his wife's devotions-only one child in 50 will become a regular worshipper. If a father does go regularly, regardless of the practice of the mother, between two-thirds and three-quarters of their children will become churchgoers (regular and irregular)."[2]

A boy who grows up believing the Bible to be true will not treat his wife poorly. The Bible has the answer to every human ill. I dare you to find one thing wrong with the following passage written by St. Paul. Would any woman object to being loved in this way?

> Husbands, love your wives, as Christ loved the church and gave himself up for her, that he might sanctify her, having cleansed her by the washing of water with the word, so that he might present the church to himself in splendor, without spot or wrinkle or any such thing, that she might be holy and without blemish. In the same way husbands should love their wives as their own bodies. He who loves his wife loves himself. For no one ever hated his own flesh, but nourishes and cherishes it, just as Christ does the church, because we are members of his body. Therefore a man shall leave his father and mother and hold fast to his wife, and the two shall become one flesh. This mystery is profound, and I am saying that it refers to Christ and the church. However, let each one of you love his wife as himself, and let the wife see that she respects her husband.[3]

Imparting traditional beliefs to our sons about sexuality is absolutely essential to keeping them from being harmed by duplicitous women. Saving sex for marriage will ensure that your son does not contract diseases, unwanted pregnancies, stalkers, and more. It may be "old-fashioned," but there are solid facts that weigh heavily on the side of chastity. Not only will an authentic Bible-believing man treat women well, but he will also value marriage, leading me to the next rule to harpyproof your son.

GET MARRIED AND STAY MARRIED

Men who get married and stay married are happier, more success-ful, and have better sex lives. Studies have shown that married men are less likely to be fired, and they typically earn ten to forty percent more than single men. The average married man in his fifties gathers over his lifetime an average of three times the assets of unmarried men in the same age group. Fifty-one percent of married men report being "extremely satisfied" with their sex lives. In comparison, only thirty-nine percent of men who are cohabitating report the same. If great sex isn't enough of a motiva-tion for you, how about longer life? Married men live an average of ten years longer than unmarried men.[4]

This is proof that God's laws really do provide for our ulti-mate good and happiness. Another very important part of marriage is staying married to the same woman. Divorce brings untold heartbreak and drama into a life that nobody wants. Family courts have devastated the lives of countless men, forcing them to pay more than they can afford, alienating them from chil-dren, and involving corrupt Child Protective Services in their lives, which can lead to the abuse of their children in foster care.

Finding the right spouse is imperative. The best way to choose a wife is to make sure you share values. Do not marry a woman who is on the opposite political spectrum. In other words, avoid SJWs like the plague. There was a time when right and left could marry and live peacefully, but that era is gone as evidenced by the rash of women divorcing their Trump-supporting husbands for no other reason than political disagreement. Leftist women generally hate men and will take out all their life disappointments on the closest man. These women have no problem trapping a man through pregnancy and then taking him for everything he has. Avoid these women. In case you are wondering how to spot them, the first indicator is how many protests they go to. If your current girlfriend can be found scratching at the doors of the Supreme Court, chasing senators out of restaurants, scaling the Statue of Liberty, or screaming helplessly at the sky because her preferred candidate didn't win an election, keep looking. If you combine any of these behaviors with brightly colored hair, watch out! Various social media commenters have noticed that the more extreme color of hair a woman has (any unnatural shade of the rainbow) the more likely she is to poison your life, much like the aposematism seen in brightly colored poisonous frogs or snakes signaling to predators that it is toxic or distasteful. While completely unscientific, it does seem true. (The key to this litmus test is not just hair alone but the combination of the neon hair *with* other red flag behavior listed above.)

For a happy life, find a woman who doesn't believe in divorce, wants to care for children as a team, and works to make a better community through legal means. Studies also show that marrying earlier leads to more stable and long-lasting marriages. People who marry in their twenties have a lower divorce rate than those who marry in their thirties. One of the reasons for this is that the longer you stay single the more rigid you become in your habits and enjoy living alone. It becomes more difficult to integrate someone into your life the longer you wait. Conversely, marrying young allows you to "grow up" with your spouse. I've been married eighteen years, and my husband and I were both twenty-four when we tied the knot. Now that we are in our forties, we look back on ourselves as kids in awe that we made it this far but can't imagine life apart because we've spent so much of it together. We literally grew up together, struggling in apartments with several jobs to make ends meet. We share so many memories of life together, and it has made us stronger. The older I get the less I can remember life without him.

LIVE BY THE MIKE PENCE RULES

Everybody laughed at quaint Mike Pence when it was discovered that he refuses to be in a room alone with a woman who is not his wife. *How old-fashioned!* the harpies on the View cackled. *Those stupid Christians are such prudes.* A few months later, the #MeToo movement took over the world and toppled Harvey Weinstein and others who didn't have the foresight to be smart enough to avoid even the appearance of scandal.

Evangelicals like Pence are mocked for their careful personal behavior, but guess who wasn't caught in any embarrassing, pants-around-the-ankles #MeToo scandal? Suddenly, the old fuddy-duddy looked like a silver fox and was acknowledged as the smartest guy in the room. Avoiding any situation that can even appear to be inappropriate is always good practice. These days, it's necessary.

If a man is not married, he should avoid being alone with any woman who is not his mother or sisters. This will pose dating difficulties. The days of chaperones may be making a comeback. Advise your son to only date in groups with witnesses. If that is impossible for him, make sure he knows to document any time spent alone with a woman using his technology. Take photos and videos and save them. Obviously, if your son was raised to honor the Ten Commandments, he won't be engaging in sex before marriage, but if he decides to throw caution to the wind, make sure he gets sent off to college with an armful of legal waivers and consent forms. This sounds like a joke, but it isn't. College campuses are notoriously dangerous for young men. Title IX allows any young man's college career to be destroyed on false testimony.

On college campuses, Title IX was supposed to be about equality and fairness but lowered the standard of evidence for rape allegations to "more likely than not," meaning that anyone could be easily destroyed like Matt Boermeester, who was a star football player at the University of Southern California. Boermeester was suspended and banned from campus as well as barred from seeing his girlfriend, the supposed victim. Trouble was, she denied it and claimed the two were roughhousing consensually when some do-gooder turned him into campus police for sexual harassment.

During the era of Obama, the left began to claim that rape was happening on campus at epidemic levels, and the president declared it a "crisis." After that, Obama's Department of Education's Office for Civil Rights demanded that universities fix it and prove they were doing it in writing or lose federal funding. That was all the motivation far left universities needed to start prosecuting guys wrestling with their girlfriends. The false accusations got so bad that President Trump's administration reversed the Obama era disaster by changing the standard of evidence to "clear and convincing" or "preponderance of evidence." This brings due process back to the table. However, the rabid feminists are still trying desperately to use their female privilege to accuse men of rape and be believed at any cost. This is why you must protect your son with seemingly laughable measures. It isn't a joke that college boys need to use "consent to sex" forms in order to cover their bases.

Even better than a written consent form is a video interview before and after laying out what she is agreeing to and confirming that those are the only things that happened. You may be chuckling at this idea, but it is going to become commonplace with men who aren't masochists after what happened to Brett Kavanaugh.

LeanIn.org created a survey after #MeToo took off and found that more than half of male managers are scared to work alone with or mentor a woman.[5] Their fear is totally justifiable and rational. If women are going to insist that due process be stripped from men for "their truth" to be believed, then they deserve to be passed over for safer working partners. Why would any man willingly sign up to be a patsy?

Encourage the men in your life to document every interaction with a woman that made them uncomfortable by emailing themselves the details and any witnesses to the event when it happened. These emails put a time and date stamp on the communication, and it is admissible in court as any journal entry would be.

An editorial in the *Jewish Voice* by Matt Paterson agrees with me almost to the letter in his column about the "rules for men" in the #MeToo era:

• Don't hire women. Where accusations against men are concerned, proof is no longer required, nor presumption of innocence granted. Under these circumstances, why on earth would a man hire any woman or interact with any woman in a professional setting?

• If a man must interact with a woman in a professional setting, he should do so as little as possible and always with a third and fourth party present (one of whom should be a man). Never under any circumstances should a man be alone with a female co-worker. No written communication with a woman co-worker should take place without a boss or supervisor and at least one male co-worker copied on the correspondence. Ditto with text and telephone communications.

•Do not mentor women or girls, large numbers of whom are clearly unstable, fragile creatures and God knows what they may mis-remember or mis-construe. Under these circumstances, it is not even remotely worth the risk to help a woman advance her career. Brett Kavanaugh has spent his life helping women professionally. What goodwill did it buy him?

• Dating and romance are now minefields to be traversed with extreme caution, if at all (see above re: mentoring). Forget making a move, going in for the kiss – unless you get express written consent before every move, you run the risk of being labeled a sexual predator for life.[6]

The importance of keeping text messages and communications with women is of utmost importance. I was told by a reader, after printing a column about this subject, that her son was barely saved from false sexual harassment allegations through text history. When the mom received notice from a parent that a classmate of her son's was claiming he had asked her for inappropriate photos, they were able to prove just the opposite. The girl in question had been coming on to the boy for a while without him responding. Angry about being rejected and after getting caught sending sexts, the girl lied to her parents, pointing her finger at the boy who didn't return her affection. At this point, if a man associates with a woman who isn't his wife, he's crazy.

DON'T TRUST WOMEN

By now, at this point in this text, this should be a no-brainer. Men are predisposed to trust women. After all, the first person every man learned to trust was a woman, his mother, and men with good mothers are probably at higher risk to fall into the trap of extending the benefit of the doubt to all women. *Don't do it.*

Women are not trustworthy simply because they carry two X chromosomes. Each person, male or female, is equally capable of doing evil. Accept that fact and act accordingly. It's unfortunate we've come to a place in history where men and women must necessarily distrust one another. Our system of government, properly functioning, eliminates that by the rule of law. "Innocent until proven guilty," when applied would weed out most of the false accusers and give people a sense that justice was done.

Withholding judgment until evidence is presented used to signal a wise individual and society. As half of the country has let go of those principles, choosing instead to disdain America's great documents and traditions, we've devolved into a hellish chaos where no one, and nothing is safe.

HOW TO HARPYPROOF YOUR DAUGHTER

$\mathcal{I}$t isn't just sons we need to inoculate, but daughters, too. If you don't want your daughter growing up to be a false accuser, then there are some things you need to do to make sure she doesn't turn into a duplicitous deceiver or a victim. The first rule will seem repetitive but necessary.

TAKE HER TO CHURCH

Church is for everyone. As I wrote on PJ Media, "Beyond teaching girls basic morality, make sure you explain to them that **unrepentant, intentional lying is a mortal sin.** It can send them straight to Hell. It is far easier to teach morality to children when they know there are eternal (and very painful) consequences for their actions. Churches that avoid doctrine about an actual, terrifying place where souls go for eternal damnation, called Hell, will not be helpful in this regard. Teaching children not to lie is a difficult thing because it comes so naturally to them, *especially girls* (and I know because I have two of them)."[1]

Women are better liars than men. I have no scientific study to back this up, but, in my experience, this is true. Others have noticed it too. "In 'Little White Lies, Deep Dark Secrets: The Truth About Women and Deception,' Susan Shapiro Barash cites an online survey of 500 women that found females "fib about everything from love, to money, to plastic surgery. Women are also much more prone to telling 'little white lies' to try to keep from hurting someone's feelings."[2]

It is my belief that, because women tend to lie about little things, they are very practiced and become flawless in their execution of tall tales. I believe it is linked to emotional intelligence, in which women are naturally more gifted than men. We have an inborn ability to manipulate emotions. In studying my own daughters, I have noticed that they work hard at manipulating their father's emotions more so than mine. Perhaps they know it is less likely to work on me, or maybe it's just instinct. Whatever the explanation, girls can lie effectively, and if those lies are left uncorrected, they can lead to the destruction of lives.

Grounding your daughters in Church teaching and biblical examples of why lying is so deleterious to their well-being is essential. Mine react well to Bible stories, so I often pull out good stories about lying like the tale of Ananias and Sapphira who tried to cheat God out of tithes and suffered a terrible fate. The tale of the cheating tax collector Zacchaeus is a good one, too. When encountering Jesus, Zacchaeus gave back four times what he stole and repaired his life.

Proverbs says, "A truthful witness saves lives, but a false witness is deceitful."[3] There can be no better example of this than the previous chapters about the consequences of false witness. Countless lives were destroyed until someone came forward with the truth. Only then could reparations be made. It is far better to be the truthful witness than the false accuser. The two opening statements by Christine Blasey Ford and Brett Kavanaugh, side by side, offer an interesting lesson on false witness. I would encourage any parent to show those to their daughters to illustrate the gravity of what false tales can do to your life and the lives of those targeted. I don't think Dr. Ford would repeat her choices if she had the foresight to see how she would be remembered in history, do you?

TEACH HER HOW TO PARTY

Ideally, we don't want our daughters, especially when they are underage, attending any parties where there might be drinking. But having been to high school and attended those parties myself without my parents' knowledge or consent, I know that my wishes may not always be respected. It is with that in mind that I offer this advice. Beer is not the problem, drunkenness is. Being drunk opens your daughter up to dangerous situations in which her safety will be compromised. In our house, we have always shown our children what drinking responsibly looks like. My husband and I drink wine with dinner sometimes and have cocktails on the weekend. We try to model what moderation looks like. My good friend Doug Giles, who has raised two fantastic girls, who made it into adulthood in one piece, wrote about this in *Raising Righteous and Rowdy Girls*.[4] I recommend this book for anyone with daughters: Here is some practical advice for your teen girls, who are headed out into the world with their drivers' licenses (and without you) to follow:

- **Choose a beer with a dark bottle.** Drink one (or empty it in the bathroom) and fill it up with water. When asked if you'd like another one you can say "No thanks! I just got one!" and no one will know what's in it.

- **Give them a code text or phrase they can use to get out of a sticky situation.** Make sure they know that if they are out doing something that breaks your rules but they need help that they can call or text you with a code phrase (some people just use one letter like "Q"), and you will immediately call their phone with a fake family emergency and extract her from the event. You will also not bring down the parental hammer on her for disobeying your rules. Instead, you will take her home, tuck her in safely and pray a prayer of thanksgiving that she is safe. The next day, you will talk about what happened with her in a calm way and let her come to the conclusion that her choices could have been better and thank her for doing the right thing. (This also works for sons, too, by the way.)

- **Teach her how to dress.** Feminists hate this advice and claim that it's "slut shaming," but my daughters are going to know what it means to respect themselves. It doesn't mean booty shorts and cleavage. As Christians, we are to be wise and not foolish. It is foolish for teen girls to traipse around at night at parties wearing next to nothing. Men will see them as easy prey, and the whole point of training young girls to be women of value is to present that impression to the world. Choosing to dress modestly may not keep a girl from being raped, but it will attract less negative attention. Camille Paglia, my favorite feminist, had this to say on the subject, "Misled by the naive optimism and 'You go, girl!' boosterism of their upbringing, young women do not see the animal eyes glowing at them in the dark. They assume that bared flesh and sexy clothes are just a fashion statement containing no messages that might be misread and twisted by a psychotic. They do not understand the fragility of civilization and the constant nearness of savage nature."[5] Teach them that self-defense includes fashion choices.

- **Don't mess around with men before**

marriage. God bless my mother for trying to tell me that. She was right, but I had to learn it the hard way, being me. I pray my girls will believe me when I tell them that playing around with men you're not going to marry is a waste of youth, time, and energy. None of those dalliances can compare to the man they will marry. And when they do find him, if there's a string of lovers behind them, there will be regret. Those church rules, if followed, lead to good things! Chastity is wise. It saves us from entanglements we might not want to be involved in. It protects hearts from breaking, diseases from spreading, regret from forming, and unwanted pregnancies from happening. The old "they're going to do it anyway" defense is still not an excuse for parents to lower expectations. Girls need to know all the ways that premature sexual activity can impact their lives negatively. Don't leave it up to the school to impart its dangerous secular philosophy to your girls. Everyone makes their own mistakes but some can be avoided. Sex too early and outside of marriage has far more cons than pros.

Honestly, is there one positive thing that can come from your daughter racking up sexual partners, as *Teen Vogue* would suggest, like she's trying to outdo Caligula? *Teen Vogue* put out an article for fifteen-year-old girls about how to have anal sex! What in the hell is going on here? (Shortly after I reported that story, *Teen Vogue* stopped production. *Hallelujah!*)[6] There are so many messages targeting teen girls to act like debauched hookers risking serious injury and illness that someone has to step in and scream, "WHY?" For orgasms? Learning self-control will benefit girls far more in every situation in life than any orgasm. Humans are not their sexuality! Instead, teach her to own her sexuality and direct it appropriately so she is not a slave to any impulse or passion. This will benefit her far more than learning how to stick things in her butt. (It's amazing I even have to write these words. I feel like we live in a live-action role play of *The Onion*.) Another reason to encourage waiting is to limit the instances where your daughter will feel pressured and experience regret. These days, regret is often miscategorized as rape because campus politicos say that a woman can retroactively retract consent if she feels icky about her choices in the morning. That's pure bunkum. Regret is a natural reaction to poor decisions. Don't let your daughters avoid regret. Teach them that the feeling of regret is the conscience's way of imparting wisdom and correction. Regret should be the catalyst to repentance and change. It is not an invitation to accuse someone of rape. If your daughter does decide to sleep around and regrets it, make sure she knows that's on her and no one else.

TEACH HER TO FIGHT

Self-defense is a human right. Gone are the days of chivalry. It is an almost certain fact that if your daughter is attacked, even if there are crowds of people nearby, all of them will film it on their mobile phones instead of helping. It is therefore necessary that today's women learn to fight. My choice of self-defense training for my girls is jiu jitsu. I prefer this martial art to others because it is based on the fact that all fights go to the ground, and once you are there, you need to know how to get away. Karate seems useless to me because all fights are done standing up. What rapist do you know is going to spar with your daughter? He's going to tackle her, probably from behind, and she needs to know how to wrestle and use his strength against him. This is what jiu jitsu teaches. Gracie jiu jitsu also has an excellent "bully-proof" training that teaches children how to avoid fights when possible but how to win if a physical confrontation is unavoidable. It's an excellent program. These days, schools cannot be counted on to protect your child from a bully, and it's an age-old wisdom that bullies don't pick on targets who can fight back. Whatever defense training you choose, choose one and keep them in it as long as you can so that fighting back becomes second nature.

TEACH HER TO SHOOT

Obviously the greatest equalizer between men and women is a gun. Gun ownership and proficiency with firearms is an excellent defense against rapists. This advice is not popular with half the country, but I would prefer my girls live. Training is essential. There is no point in carrying a firearm if you don't know how to use it properly. My husband has been teaching our daughters to shoot since they were four. They're pretty good at it now. Both of them have been hunting with their dad and see guns as useful tools that come with rules. I trust my children around guns. Both of them know how to load, unload, check if a gun is loaded, and are well-versed in safety. We also bought them Red Ryder BB guns for Christmas when they each turned eight, and they love going into the woods with them and target shooting to this day. When they are of age, they will take the state training to carry concealed. I refuse to send them to college unarmed. There's no point in making girls afraid of guns unless you don't want them to be able to defend their lives. Evil exists, and one day it may meet your daughter in a dark alley or on a date. I hope she's packing if that happens.

TEACH HER TO SEEK JUSTICE

Teach your daughter that she is not a victim. She is entitled to justice, and, if the worst happens and she is raped, she needs to know that the worst thing she can do is stay silent and wait thirty years to tell anyone. If she waits and the statute of limitations runs out, there's nothing that can be done. Further, even if there is no statute of limitations, any evidence will have grown cold or been destroyed and the possibility of holding someone accountable is virtually zero. Many girls do not come forward because they are afraid of the consequences for breaking rules they shouldn't have broken. Let your girls know that nothing they were doing would prevent you from seeking justice against a legitimate attack. The advice above about extracting them from uncomfortable situations should solve the issue of them lying to you to cover their tracks. If they know you won't be angry with them for breaking your rules, they won't have a reason to lie. Girls must be taught these things early. Have frank conversations with them about how our legal system works. Here are the rules of dealing with sexual assault:

- Fight like hell to get away, and, if that fails, try to scratch and claw at the attacker to preserve DNA under fingernails.
- After an assault, the very first thing to do is get to a safe place then call the police and parents.
- *Do not shower or change clothes or even wash hands.* Evidence must be preserved.
- Get to a hospital for a rape kit as soon as possible.
- Do not be afraid to name the attacker if he is familiar. It's tough to imagine that a relative or someone close to the family could be a rapist, but it happens frequently. Over 70% of rapes are committed by someone known to the victim.[7] Make sure your daughter knows she can tell you anything.
- Also make sure she knows that if she does delay in coming forward, and does not do these things listed above, that her story will be suspect, and you will consider that she may have lied. Hopefully, the lessons you taught her about the severity of lying and its consequences will have eliminated that possibility.

To quote my favorite columnist (me), "Make sure you tell her that if she does not come forward, every day she waits is another day further away from justice until the day comes when justice cannot be had. Don't wait for that day. Do it now. The only way women will overcome sexual assault is to become bold and courageous, and the only place to learn that is in the home. Parents, it is your job to keep your daughters from becoming victims — or victimizers. And what a tough job it is."[8]

CONCLUSION

The withholding of due process from one set of people and not others, helped by the fake news media, can and will spark a civil war if it does not stop. The media has painted a world for the left where they are victims of crimes by villains in red hats, creating scores of MAGAphobes who can and do commit violence against Trump supporters. It matters not that all of it is false. All that matters to the lying media is political victory and helping Democrats win elections. They do not care how many people are harmed, how many buildings are burned, how many windows are smashed, or how many commuters are stopped by mass protests on highways. These things are all peripheral to the fake news media whose one goal is to elect more Democrats. The collateral damage done to Americans by these gangsters of chaos is meaningless to them.

Even their so-called support of women is counterfeit and only designed to harm perceived enemies. Republican women will never get the kind of backing the media offers women who harm their enemies, or be taken at their word for any reason. Paula Jones, Juanita Broderick, and the rest of Bill Clinton's accusers weren't even Republicans, but their stories threatened a Democrat, and so they were not believed; their stories were not pushed as true, and as a result they were demonized and destroyed by a rabid press willing to do the Democrats' bidding.

In order to combat the massive damage being done to Americans at the hands of the press and political operatives, the people of this country need to embrace due process and demand that our media stop reporting allegations as fact. Any news outlet that does this before an investigation is completed should be ridiculed mercilessly for engaging in journalistic malpractice and lose its license. Major news media outlets are taking items generally reserved for a police blotter column and making major headlines out of them. How is this allowed by editorial staff, and why don't the American people demand that it stop?

Lives are ruined, families destroyed, and careers ended by the blatant disregard for our laws and processes and it must stop now. #BelieveWomen is just a cover for political shenanigans aimed at silencing and harming conservatives. Women are no more trustworthy than men, as this book has shown, and it's past time for us to profess a new Declaration of Independence from a corrupt and tyrannical press.

From this day on, we will only believe evidence!

ACKNOWLEDGMENTS

This book could not have happened without the support of many people. My husband is first on the list for putting up with far too many dinners of frozen pizza and cold sandwiches and wrangling three kids into bed on his own without complaining. Jason Rennie of Superversive Press believed that this book was in me and took a chance that it wasn't. L. Jagi Lamplighter stepped in at the last minute and gave me great feedback and advice. Deplora Boule, my soul-sister, and dear friend, without whose direction and help I may not have ever published anything. My cabal of closeted creatives (you know who you are) cheered me on and inspired me every day. Daniella Bova, founder of the only "safe-space" I ever want to be in, talked me off the ledge repeatedly and prayed for me always. The professionals in the Conservative-Libertarian Fiction Alliance never failed to answer a question, offer assistance, or hurl a well-phrased insult. Kia Heavey and

Marina Fontaine have their hands full moderating that unruly bunch, but they do it with style. Matt Margolis, cover designer and formatting wizard, who managed to pull me over the finish line, is a god among men. My Auntie Annie, who got me my first writing gig and refused to let inferior technology derail me, is the reason I have a working computer and a career. My mom and dad kept this book under wraps for many months (which was hard because they are my superfans.) Tucker Carlson of Fox News gave my column, "How to Christine Blasey Ford-Proof Your Son," the spotlight, launching this project. Kevin DuJan, my fearless partner in mystery-solving and wild adventures, urged me to write that column in the first place. My family at PJ Media, especially Paula Bolyard, my long suffering editor, without whom I can't function (or punctuate anything properly), was patient when I disappeared for weeks at a time. To every reader who has been with me over the years and the new ones, too, without you, none of this was possible, and I thank you and bless you for your support.

ABOUT THE AUTHOR

Megan Fox is an award-winning journalist, author, and columnist at PJ Media. Her books included "Shut Up! The bizarre war
that one public library waged on the First Amendment," "Fighting
for My Children's Future," a compilation work of *PJ Media*
authors about homeschooling and "To Be Men," an anthology on
manliness by Superversive Press authors. Fox is a devout
Catholic, a former homeschooling mom and parents' rights advocate. She lives in an undisclosed location with her husband, three
children, giant German Shepherd, "Moose," fourteen chickens and
two guinea pigs.

ENDNOTES

INTRODUCTION

1. https://twitter.com/AnnCoulter/status/1045402229061144579
2. https://pjmedia.com/trending/when-every-boy-is-guilty-every-girl-becomes-a-monster/

1. EVE

1. Genesis 2:22-23 ESV

2. ATHALIA

1. 2Kings 11:1-3 ESV
2. Leviticus 20: 1-5 ESV
3. https://www.guttmacher.org/journals/psrh/2005/reasons-us-women-have-abortions-quantitative-and-qualitative-perspectives
4. https://www.cdc.gov/mmwr/preview/mmwrhtml/00041486.htm#00001660.htm
5. https://www.prnewswire.com/news-releases/americans-support-supreme-court-ruling-to-restrict-abortion-oppose-taxpayer-funding-300394731.html

3. JEZEBEL

1. Matthew 7:3-5 ESV
2. 1 Kings 21:8-14 ESV
3. 2 Kings 9:30-35 ESV
4. https://www.mediaite.com/tv/watch-kavanaugh-accuser-julie-swetnick-back-tracks-on-some-claims-in-extensive-nbc-news-interview/

4. POTIPHAR'S WIFE

1. Genesis 41:37-45 ESV

5. SALOME

1. https://pjmedia.com/lifestyle/2017/09/28/anal-cancer-new-gay-epidemic-media-wont-talk/
2. http://www.nbcnews.com/id/24036106/ns/health-womens_health/t/eww-factor-aside-anal-hpv-infection-risk/#.Wcxg7NOGN-U
3. https://pjmedia.com/lifestyle/2017/09/28/anal-cancer-new-gay-epidemic-media-wont-talk/
4. https://www.churchmilitant.com/news/article/the-catholic-magazine-inter-view-with-milo-they-refuse-to-print
5. Matthew 14:1-12 ESV
6. Catholic Catechism (2348-2349)
7. Catholic Catechism (2340-2342)

6. LADY MACBETH

1. https://www.dailymail.co.uk/news/article-3566662/Michigan-woman-44-convicted-1999-love-triangle-murder-husband-ADMITS-killing-maintaining-innocence-16-years.html
2. https://www.guttmacher.org/fact-sheet/induced-abortion-united-states
3. Isaiah 5:20-21 ESV

7. ABIGAIL WILLIAMS

1. Miller, Arthur. *The Crucible*. Introduction, Bigsby, Christopher. New York: Penguin Group, 1995.
2. https://www.dailywire.com/news/36997/witchcraft-spells-being-cast-follow-ing-kavanaugh-paul-bois
3. https://www.npr.org/2018/09/26/651940992/read-brett-kavanaughs-open-ing-statement-for-senate-hearing
4. https://www.youtube.com/watch?v=4ccXpDhMmBY

5. Miller, Arthur. *The Crucible*. New York: Penguin Group, 1995.

6. https://dailycaller.com/2018/09/30/usa-today-column-kavanaugh-youth-basketball/

8. MAYELLA VIOLET EWELL

1. Lee, Harper. *To Kill a Mockingbird*, New York, NY. HarperCollins Publishers, 1960.

2. https://lithub.com/mia-the-liberal-men-we-love/?fbclid=IwAR01zxtgu-LJ1RKapwORaMN4z0P1oc2XC-17eFxGCTHXnKTz96KyW4hssoqI

3. https://www.washingtonpost.com/outlook/2018/10/12/thanks-not-raping-us-all-you-good-men-its-not-enough/?utm_term=.389c09670e67

9. VICTORIA PRICE AND RUBY BATES

1. Goodman, James. Stories of Scottsboro, Vintage Books, New York, NY, 1994 pg. 171

2. Goodman, pg.26

3. Goodman, pg.36

4. Goodman, pg.42

5. Goodman, pg.44

10. TAWANA BRAWLEY

1. https://www.youtube.com/watch?v=T78DwdFUq0c

2. https://www.nytimes.com/1988/09/27/nyregion/evidence-points-to-deceit-by-brawley.html?pagewanted=all

3. https://www.nytimes.com/1988/09/27/nyregion/evidence-points-to-deceit-by-brawley.html?pagewanted=all

4. https://pjmedia.com/trending/sen-kennedy-to-feinstein-you-should-hide-your-head-in-a-bag/

11. CRYSTAL GAIL MANGUM

1. Taylor Jr., Stuart. *Until Proven Innocent: Political Correctness and the Shameful Injustices of the Duke Lacrosse Rape Case* (Kindle Locations 651-655). St. Martin's Press. Kindle Edition
2. Stuart, (Kindle Locations 679-686).
3. Stuart, (Kindle Locations 697-701)
4. Stuart, (Kindle Locations 706-708)
5. https://www.huffpost.com/entry/mom-angry-that-teacher-wo_b_5882764
6. Stuart, (Kindle Locations 738-744)
7. http://www.washingtonpost.com/wp-dyn/content/article/2006/12/30/AR2006123000886.html?referrer=emailarticle&noredirect=on
8. Stuart, (Kindle Locations 912-914
9. https://www.smh.com.au/sport/bonded-in-barbarity-when-fear-of-ridicule-overrides-all-20060401-gdnaa3.html
10. https://nypost.com/2007/01/18/orwell-university-duke-profs-p-c-travesty/

12. KERRI DUNN

1. http://www.newsrealblog.com/2010/12/20/top-10-hoaxes-perpetrated-by-the-left-and-trumpeted-by-a-complicit-media-1/2/

13. DR. LYNNE SNOWDEN

1. https://www.amazon.com/Welcome-Ivory-Tower-Babel-Conservative/dp/1891799177/ref=sr_1_2?ie=UTF8&qid=1540439916&sr=8-2&keywords=the+ivory+tower+of+babel
2. https://townhall.com/columnists/mikeadams/2005/04/20/bigmouth-at-monmouth-n1279763
3. Adams, Mike S., *Welcome to the Ivory Tower of Babel; Confessions of a Conservative Professor*. Harbor House, Augusta, GA., 2004

14. EMMA SULKOWICZ "MATTRESS GIRL"

1. https://www.nytimes.com/2014/09/22/arts/design/in-a-mattress-a-fulcrum-of-art-and-political-protest.html
2. https://www.nytimes.com/2015/05/29/magazine/have-we-learned-anything-from-the-columbia-rape-case.html
3. https://www.nationalreview.com/2017/08/columbia-university-mattress-girl-emmas-sulkowicz-paul-nungesser-lawsuit-rape-accusation-exonerated/
4. https://www.thedailybeast.com/columbia-student-i-didnt-rape-her
5. https://www.nationalreview.com/2017/08/columbia-university-mattress-girl-emmas-sulkowicz-paul-nungesser-lawsuit-rape-accusation-exonerated/
6. https://www.nationalreview.com/2017/05/mattress-girl-emma-sulkowicz-pathetic-journey-provocateur/
7. https://www.breitbart.com/entertainment/2015/06/05/mattress-girl-emma-sulkowicz-just-released-a-sex-tape-heres-my-review/

15. DINA MACKNEY

1. https://www.amazon.com/Bullied-Death-Mackneys-Kafkaesque-Divorce-ebook/dp/B0149ERBBI/ref=sr_1_1
2. https://www.avoiceformen.com/mens-rights/family-courts/i-am-chris-mackney-and-i-have-something-to-say-from-the-grave/

16. KHADIJA ALTAMIMI & YASMIN SEWEID

1. https://www.breitbart.com/the-media/2017/01/04/ann-coulter-great-hijab-cover/
2. http://www.nydailynews.com/new-york/nyc-crime/drunk-men-screaming-trump-attack-muslim-straphanger-article-1.2896163
3. http://www.nydailynews.com/new-york/muslim-woman-reported-trump-supporter-attack-made-story-article-1.2910944

17. UNIDENTIFIED LIAR IN NEW YORK

1. https://www.essence.com/news/two-black-men-exonerated-rape-victim-lied/
2. https://www.huffingtonpost.com/2013/08/20/elizabeth-coast-rape-lie_n_3784718.html
3. https://www.huffingtonpost.com/entry/breana-harmon-false-rape-jail_us_5a958207e4b03a8f3a22f390
4. https://www.wsj.com/articles/alan-m-dershowitz-a-nightmare-of-false-accusation-that-could-happen-to-you-1421280860

19. TAYLIER TIBBETS

1. https://nationalpost.com/opinion/christie-blatchford-b-c-man-blamed-cruelty-of-family-court-battle-for-driving-him-to-suicide

20. SEXUAL HARASSMENT GOES BOTH WAYS

1. https://www.psychologytoday.com/us/blog/media-spotlight/201505/when-men-face-sexual-harassment
2. https://www.dailymail.co.uk/femail/article-3491650/Male-victims-sexual-harassment-share-shocking-stories-publicly-groped-women.html
3. https://spectator.org/the-women-movements-embrace-of-psychopath-donna-hylton/

21. #METOO HYPOCRITES

1. https://www.nytimes.com/2018/12/23/us/womens-march-anti-semitism.html
2. https://www.advocate.com/women/2018/10/30/metoo-activist-alyssa-milano-wont-be-stopped?fbclid=IwAR1NS1a_HBSolO9rwBZjnbQfcBb2Is-CWHI0QTiJNtd_aKWeMbd62pT4AkAM

22. THE COVINGTON CATHOLIC BOYS

1. https://pjmedia.com/trending/diocese-of-covington-walking-back-condemnation-of-maga-kids/
2. https://www.thewrap.com/film-producer-jack-morrissey-apologizes-for-deleted-covington-woodchipper-tweet/
3. https://pjmedia.com/trending/native-american-activist-who-claimed-to-be-vietnam-vet-has-three-awols-on-his-record/
4. https://www.youtube.com/watch?v=lSkpPaiUF8s
5. https://crooksandliars.com/2019/01/details-emerge-covington-catholic-kids
6. https://twitchy.com/gregp-3534/2019/01/21/alyssa-milano-says-the-red-maga-hat-is-the-new-white-hood/
7. https://www.politico.com/magazine/story/2019/01/24/lowry-covington-maga-hats-224215
8. https://www.cnn.com/2019/01/21/opinions/maga-hat-has-become-a-potent-racist-symbol-bailey/index.html

23. HOW TO HARPYPROOF YOUR SON

1. https://www.aei.org/publication/black-men-making-it-in-america-the-engines-of-economic-success-for-black-men-in-america/
2. https://www.christianpost.com/news/fathers-key-to-their-childrens-faith-51331/
3. Ephesians 5:25-33 ESV
4. https://www.menshealth.com/sex-women/a19539817/benefits-of-being-married/
5. https://leanin.org/sexual-harassment-backlash-survey-results
6. http://thejewishvoice.com/2018/10/04/metoo-new-rules-men/

24. HOW TO HARPYPROOF YOUR DAUGHTER

1. https://pjmedia.com/parenting/how-to-christine-blasey-ford-proof-your-daughter/
2. https://www.cbsnews.com/news/author-women-lie-more-better-than-men/
3. Proverbs 14:25 ESV

4. https://www.amazon.com/gp/product/0983175128
5. http://time.com/3444749/camille-paglia-the-modern-campus-cannot-comprehend-evil/
6. https://pjmedia.com/parenting/teen-vogue-shutters-shortly-publishing-guide-anal-sex-teen-girls/
7. https://www.rainn.org/
8. https://pjmedia.com/parenting/how-to-christine-blasey-ford-proof-your-daughter/

9 798606 379491